LIFE AWAKENING

THE WORKBOOK

LIFE AWAKENING
THE WORKBOOK

THE UNIQUE, MIND-BODY-SPIRIT SOULISTIC LIFE REVIEW PROGRAMME

Miriam Grace & Jillian Schofield

Soulistic Publications, a subsection of Soulistic Therapy 2014
Derby, UK.

Printed by CreateSpace, An Amazon.com Company
CreateSpace, Charleston SC
CreateSpace

Soulistic Publications
ISBN-13: 978-1503129962

CONTENTS OVERVIEW

PREFACE

*'It is better to live your own destiny imperfectly than to live an imitation
of somebody else's life with perfection.'*
Anonymous, The Bhagavad Gita

The Human Trinity Principles (HTP) are the creation of two long-term, experienced psychotherapists and lecturers in psychological therapy. The Principles, their discovery, research base, evolution and practice are all explained within *Life Awakening* (working title) a book to be published in 2015 by Miriam Grace and Jillian Schofield.

HTP is a logical coming of age for psychotherapy. Just as religions have grown multi-faith centres, HTP is a multi-therapy approach and incorporates a process based on a principle which we have seen to be healing to clients and ourselves, based on the paradoxical theory of change. HTP supports people to understand and accept who they are, not to strive to be different, and in this way a great change arrives.

While writing the above book we began to run courses about the Principles, using them to help others undertake a unique life review. This gave rise to exercises, meditations and eventually this workbook. This workbook is based on the middle section of *Life Awakening*. The importance of the concepts and why they work is explained within the *Life Awakening* book.

The Human Trinity Principles concept is like a tree with many branches; HTP therapy, HTP life review, HTP meditation groups, HTP training courses, HTP for depression, HTP approach to personality and a planned series of books are all branches of this tree. In 2014 this tree is a strong and healthy seedling, and the potential for a long period of growth is ahead of it. The focus for 2014 is the Life Awakening Life Review courses, workshops and tutorials, moving towards publishing our core book in 2015. We are also structuring courses for personal development and professional development, in order that there will be more HTP practitioners around the globe within a few years.

*'Change occurs when one becomes what he is, not when he tries to
become what he is not. Change does not take place through a coercive
attempt by the individual or by another person to change him, but it does
take place if one takes the time and effort to be what he is — to be fully
invested in his current positions.'*
Arnold Beisser, M.D. (1970)

ACKNOWLEDGEMENTS

Our thanks and respect go to our original participants and case study clients and those who attended the first HTP workshop days and sessions. We couldn't have done this without your enthusiasm, feedback and support in this endeavour. When we were at our 'is this really a good idea?' stage, you kept us believing.

A heartfelt thank you to Catherine McMann our copy-editor and proofreader.

A huge thank you to David Barnes for his illustrations and to Ben White for the designs.

We would like to recognise and fully appreciate the patience of our families as we went through this journey.

INTRODUCTION

What if you had the opportunity to review a project half way through rather than at the end? What if that project were you?

The **Life Awakening** life review with the **Human Trinity Principles** (HTP) is a process that appeals to all those who can see the benefit of reviewing the most important project – your life – before the end, while there is time to understand your unique path.

This book will help you to go over your 'original product design', the development of your self in life, problems and patterns, to the current phase of the project; to review and to put the work back on track! The model was written by two therapists who bring to the programme the depth of psychotherapy, the breadth of bodywork and the height of spiritual development. You can bring a diverse panel of specialists to reflect on and consider this most important project review of all – yourself.

The Human Trinity is mind, body and spirit. During the Life Review we view our unique **Birth Gifts** (we view these through 7 lenses), our **Life Patterns** and themes and our current expression of **Now** (using enneagram, Myers Briggs and Chinese medicine among approaches). All three stages are looked at through the Trinity. By using different perspectives and lenses to look at ourselves and seeing how all three aspects of ourselves (mind, body, spirit) link together, we are able to gain a clearer picture and insight from what we call the **Viewing Platform**.

In the story of the Blind Men and the Elephant, six blind men describe the elephant, as they can feel her, from their perspective; she is described as a fan, a tree, a wall, a snake and so on. Only by sharing many different views can they see the whole elephant. This book helps you look from many perspectives, through many different 'lenses' in order to gain a more complete picture of who you are. The 'expert panel' is yourself and any specialist you wish to include in the process, the programme gives you plenty of views for you to explore at the depth you wish.

HTP doesn't endorse, argue for, or push the beliefs of these systems upon you, whether psychoanalytic thinking, astrological knowledge or ancient Chinese wisdom; you will learn that the course is about not being afraid to look at yourself from various perspectives. What you make of the different views or perspectives of you is centred around using your **Inner Voice** to discern. Engaging left and right brain thinking, being creative, being a researcher, being a little bit 'out there' are all aspects of study you are encouraged to undertake, without either disregarding or adopting. Above all this is a fun and growthful adventure, a true experience of open eyes and open mind.

The Life Awakening Process

This workbook is unique in that the content is in you!

This workbook is a process, a guide, for you to follow to enable YOU to access your life. It is simply written, and the amount of complexity, detail and research within it is up to you. It's all in you. The deeper you go, the more you fill in, reflect and connect with your Inner Voice, then the fuller your book will be with specialist knowledge about yourself.

Opening your eyes, opening your mind

The beginning of waking up to your life is opening your eyes. This workbook and the workshops that inspired it are designed to do just that, to help you open your eyes to who you are.

You have happened upon this workbook, maybe you are lucky enough to be enrolled on one of our programmes, maybe you are interested in working through the workbook at home.

> *Either way you hold in your hands one of the clues to your life*
> *– your desire, your wish, your turning point for life awakening.*

You have chosen to open your eyes more fully today, to wake up to more than the day ahead, to wake up to your self within. As well as opening your eyes we will be asking you to open your mind to a variety of possibilities.

This workbook shows you how to use the Human Trinity Principles to chart your own destiny and then fulfil it.

From researching and charting your Birth Gifts, journaling your Life Themes and Patterns and assessing your current Now experiences, you will be guided through the process of an HTP assessment, which you can undertake at home with this workbook or in conjunction with an HTP workshop or therapy programme. All three stages of your life are looked at through the Trinity. By using different perspectives and lenses to look at ourselves, and seeing how all three aspects of ourselves (Mind-Body-Spirit) link together, we are able to gain a clearer picture and insight from the HTP Viewing Platform.

The Human Trinity model is Mind-Body-Spirit trinity. You may be quite surprised that a psychologically-based therapy incorporates pre-psychoanalytic methods of exploring and defining personality, such as tarot or astrology. This is because whether we like it or not we are constantly using labels about ourselves including psychological labels (for example, anxious, depressed, neurotic). By exploring metaphor and archetype, even gods and goddess, we encourage therapist and client alike to use right and left brain function, creativity and intelligent analysis, in order to loosen the constraints of restrictive thought processes that may not be helpful.

The Human Trinity Principles

The Human Trinity Principles are based on the concept that we are made up of Mind-Body-Spirit and that therapy is quicker, more permanent and effective when all three aspects are worked with.

HTP aims to help the individual explore and come closer to an understanding of their own unique 'make and model'. We need to understand and see the unique individual.

It is client-centred, in that the person's uniqueness and choice is honoured; yet it goes beyond that, by offering views outside the client's perspective in order to stimulate them to think 'outside the box'. By working with archetype (dreams, goddess, astrology, enneagram and so on) or finding our type (Chinese medicine, Ayurvedic medicine, Myers Briggs or even psychiatric terms) we can choose to use labels not to *define* ourselves but to *explore* ourselves.

HTP does not consider one therapeutic discipline as superior to another, it works to help strengthen the individual's Inner Voice so that they can choose and discern for themselves which direction they wish to take, and which therapeutic or personal development perspective they wish to deepen.

As HTP has a strong self-empowerment, self-help basis, this can make therapy assessment or Life Review safer and more contained. We believe that people know what is best for themselves and who they truly are. However their life may have given them different messages or they have lost who they are.

Do you have a pile of discarded self-help books beside your bed?
We don't believe in self-improvement, it doesn't work unless it is your true soul's longing. Find out about your unique path, forget who other people told you to be and embrace being you with joy. Do you want to find out more about your uniqueness? Then let's begin….

How to Use this Workbook

This workbook and course are in your hands. You can work at the depth and the speed you wish. In many ways it is true that the more you put in, the more you get out. Please consider what meets your needs; you may want to review your life quickly or deeply. If you listen to your Inner Voice now and throughout you will know what is right for you.

Self-responsibility

This course and book are not a substitute for any medical intervention or psychotherapeutic intervention which may be needed. Please take responsibility for your own mental and physical health and ensure you have the support you need in place. The course at depth can be an emotional journey, and you may find journaling and writing is good for you, or you may wish to have additional support. At all times, just as with physical exercises, if the exercises hurt, or are too difficult, discontinue; if they stretch you and you can feel it, that's fine!

Support

Throughout this book there are many exercises for you to undertake to explore your Birth Gifts, Life Patterns and where you are Now. These guidelines are to help you undertake the work in a way that is safe and manageable.

A key concept in the Human Trinity Principles process is the Viewing Platform. This is important because it keeps us in a non-judgemental observational position. It is also very important because it supports us to look at difficult things in our lives without re-traumatising.

If you engage in the workshop programme you will have a personal tutor for questions about the materials and you can always arrange individual therapy sessions with an HTP practitioner or other practitioner of your own choosing.

Previous Trauma Notes

This is a life review; if you have experienced trauma in your life that still affects you and that you have not yet integrated you may become re-traumatised. Therefore it is recommended that if this is the case, you work through this guide with a therapist or a support person, who will help you if you need therapy.

If you have integrated previous traumas then the course guidelines to stay on the Viewing Platform, to self-monitor and listen to your Inner Voice, are very important to help you enjoy the process.

If you have had therapy before you may be used to engaging with your feelings. Do remember this life review is not therapy. There is no merit in cathartic work during the review, and we advise you to stay on the Viewing Platform.

Icons and What They Mean

 Undertake the Viewing Platform meditation.

 Meditate using the Inner Voice.

 Write in your journal.

 Go online.

 Reflect on your Trinity balance.

 Read.

 Complete a worksheet.

 Consider if you need some support, to talk to a friend, or a therapist, or get a hug from someone.

Practical Information

Email:
jillian.a.schofield@gmail.com
miriam@blue-skies.org.uk

Website Information:
www.blue-skies.org.uk
www.soulistic-therapy.co.uk

Life Awakening Student Resource Page:
http://www.blue-skies.org.uk/student-resources/

Twitter:
Jillian Schofield @soultherapy68
Miriam Granthier @MiriamBlueSkies
Life Awakening @Life_awakening

HTP Facebook Community Page:
https://www.facebook.com/pages/Life-Awakening-with-Human-Trinity-Principles/557043871031883

Other Facebook Pages:
https://www.facebook.com/BlueSkiesMiriamGranthier
https://www.facebook.com/soulistictherapy

Just as you are unique, there are packages to fit everyone, from using this workbook yourself, intensive individual support and coaching, to home study with videos and audio clips. We run workshops, coach via Skype and face to face, and write books and materials to help people all around the world to wake up to themselves and live their life.

Preparation Exercises

Journal

       Take some time now to reflect on why you have this book in your hands right now. What has brought you to Life Review and Life Awakening? Why now? What is happening for you inside, and in your life? How do you know this is the right time for this process?

The Viewing Platform

Find a comfortable place to sit or lie down, with no distractions. Gently breathe and notice the breath arriving and departing and arriving again in its own natural rhythm and waves.

With each out breath, let the tension release.
Release from your head, your eyes, your mouth and jaw, your scalp and ears.

Let your neck become free, your shoulders become wide and open, your arms release and your fingers relax.

Breathe into your rib cage; front, back and sides.
Release your pelvis, think of it as giving you a big open smile.

Relax and release your thighs, your knees, your calves and let all the tension drain out of your feet and toes.

Bring your attention to your centre, your middle. Notice how you can always return here when your mind wanders.

Now let yourself be in your safe space. This may be a place in nature or at home where you are totally safe. Look at it and picture all the details. Notice the sounds, smells, colours of this place. This is your safe space.

Now it is time to climb up onto your Viewing Platform. Picture your steps, what are they made of? And count the seven steps as you climb; One, two, three, four, five, six, seven.

What is your Viewing Platform made of? Where do you like to sit? Do you notice that you have a companion or guide with you up on the platform? This may be a person, an animal, an angel or someone else.

Remember you may like to be there alone or you may like a companion with you; a safe person, an animal, an angel or a guide. At all times remember you are watching your life from your Viewing Platform and you can return to your safe place at any time down the seven steps.

At the end of the exercise when guided, count as you climb down, Seven, six, five, four, three, two, one and as you arrive in your safe place again, begin to notice your breath, the movement of your rib cage, notice your fingers and toes and when you are ready gently bring yourself back to you.

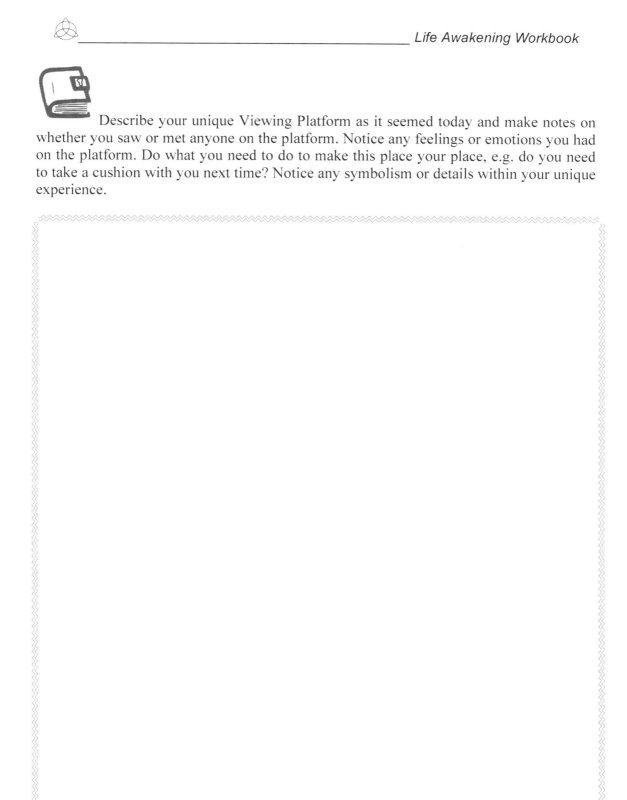

Describe your unique Viewing Platform as it seemed today and make notes on whether you saw or met anyone on the platform. Notice any feelings or emotions you had on the platform. Do what you need to do to make this place your place, e.g. do you need to take a cushion with you next time? Notice any symbolism or details within your unique experience.

Accessing Your Inner Voice

Find a comfortable place to sit or lie down, with no distractions. Gently breathe and notice the breath arriving and departing and arriving again in its own natural rhythm and waves.

With each out breath, let the tension release.
Release from your head, your eyes, your mouth and jaw, your scalp and ears.

Let your neck become free, your shoulders become wide and open, your arms release and your fingers relax.

Breathe into your rib cage; front, back and sides.
Release your pelvis, think of it as giving you a big open smile.

Relax and release your thighs, your knees, your calves and let all the tension drain out of your feet and toes.

Bring your attention to your centre, your middle. Notice how you can always return here when your mind wanders.

Now imagine you are at a harbour, selecting a boat to travel. When you find your boat, notice what it is made of, how it looks, whether there is writing on it, whether you will travel alone. As you travel across the water consider the question or questions that you seek guidance for. As you come to an island, with a hill on it, moor your boat and climb the hill. Notice the sounds, the smells, the colours. Notice if the path is easy or difficult. At the top of the hill is a sacred building, examine the building and go inside, leaving your shoes outside the door.

In the centre of the building is a mirror and when you look in the mirror you see a wise woman or wise man gazing back at you. Ask this person your question and take time to hear what they say.

As you leave to go they give you a symbol or a gift to represent the response they gave you. You thank them. You put on your shoes, descend from the hill, climb aboard your boat and travel across water reflecting on all you have learned. When you arrive in the harbour you look at the symbol or gift. You visualise this somewhere in your home, the place you live now. And slowly, gently open your eyes.

Inner Voice Access - Quick Version!

> *Close your eyes. In your mind, write your question on a piece of paper and drop it down the well inside you. See it float down. Await an answer patiently and pay attention to whatever emerges.*

There are many quick access versions; you may already have one of your own, or be used to prayer or meditation practice. A combination of longer time and quick moments of connection with your Inner Voice each day will make access quicker and easier over time.

How familiar are you with your Inner Voice? Take time to note down here how easy or difficult it is to trust your Inner Voice. Ask yourself how you could improve this relationship with your Inner Voice and what you could do. Ask your Inner Voice to be with you and guide you in your work on this course. You could even create a saying or phrase that you use when you particularly want to connect with Inner Voice wisdom. Ask your Inner Voice what your phrase might be.

Overview of the Life Awakening Process

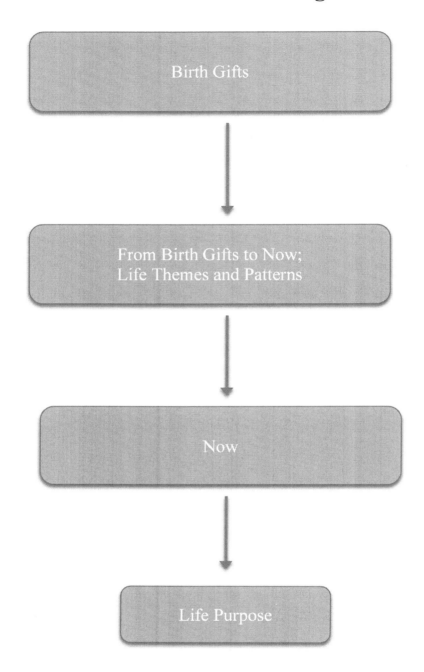

PART ONE: BIRTH GIFTS

Contents

The Seven Lenses
      Numerology
      Birth Cards
      Astrology
      Chinese Horoscope
      Ancestors & Family
      Historical & Cultural
      Physical Gifts

Summary of Birth Gifts

PART ONE
BIRTH GIFTS

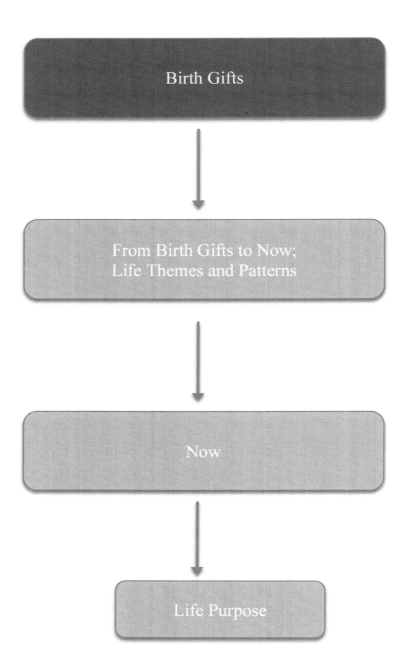

PART ONE

BIRTH GIFTS

Imagine being handed a beautifully wrapped present, complete with ribbon, on a great occasion such as your birthday! Today is the day to unwrap a whole pile of presents and gifts; your Birth Gifts!

In the beginning…
To start this amazing journey we first need to explore when you were born and the family and culture you were born into.

You may know some of the information, or if you can, you may want to ask members of your family for their memories. It could be a reason to contact people; so often as people get older we only see our extended family at weddings and funerals. People enjoy talking about themselves so go and ask them.

When we explore our Birth Gifts we start with what we are born with from a wider perspective than just the family of origin; we look at different ways people have interpreted the gifts we are born with, using numerology, tarot cards and astrology for example.

The Seven Lenses

We have identified seven lenses to look through to help you identify your Birth Gifts, and there are many more lenses if you choose to go deeper into your exploration.

The seven lenses we have chosen for this Life Review are:
- Numerology
- Birth Cards
- Astrology
- Chinese Astrology
- Ancestors & Family
- Culture & Context
- Physical Gifts

We start in the areas related to your birth date and birth name (numerology, birth cards and astrology) then move into the context of what you were born into.

Let's get started….

Numerology

The first Birth Gift we explore is numerology.

Numerology has a very long, broad history. It is considered as one of the earliest forms of metaphysical reading and communication, with evidence of it being used in China, Italy, Japan, India and Greece thousands of years ago. Mayans and Incas both employed number systems to gain a deeper understanding of themselves and the universe.

The theory is that the universe vibrates at its own frequency, so by finding its vibration you can establish the qualities and energies associated with it. Applying the principle of numerology to a person's birth name and date can determine the frequencies of a person.

It can be used to determine a person's personality, strengths and talents, obstacles, inner needs and emotional reactions. It is said that we can use numerology to identify what our mission is upon this plane by analysing our full name and birth date. 'According to numerology wherever our name came from, it is an inclusion of the characteristics, talents and ability which we have acquired in the last plane' (Riley & Balliett 1996).

The way we use numerology in an HTP assessment is to explore the idea of life mission and the characteristics we would be seen to be born with to help carry out the 'mission'.

**Jill says:** To give you an idea I will share my results. My full name is Jillian Ann Schofield and the results show a character number of 6, a soul urge number of 4 and an inner dream number of 11. What does that mean? I have included the meanings below.

Jill's example

Character number 6	The number 6 provides a sense of responsibility, love, and balance.
	People with character number 6 are helpful and conscientious. They can balance inharmonious situations.
	They may have creative and artistic talents, however they are more likely to devote themselves to an occupation that shows concern for the betterment of the community.
	The positive side of the number 6 suggests that these people are very loving, friendly, and appreciative of others, with a depth of understanding that produces sympathy, kindness, and generosity. Openness and honesty is apparent in their approach to all relationships.
	The more difficult side of a 6 is that there may be a tendency for these people to be too exacting and demanding of themselves and as such may at times sacrifice themselves (or loved ones) for the welfare of others.

Soul number 4	With the soul urge number of 4 you are likely to strive for a stable life and follow a rather orderly pattern and systematic approach. There is the inner desire to serve others in a methodical and diligent manner, to be in solid, conventional, and well-regulated activities. Excellent at organising, systematising, and managing, they have a way of establishing order and maintaining it. They are responsible, reliable and practical. Highly analytical, they can see their way through all sorts of situations and have a clear understanding of the issues. They are very honest, sincere, and conscientious individuals. The more difficult side of the 4 is rigid, stubborn and somewhat narrow-minded, with a tendency to hide feelings, or to really not be aware of real feelings.
Inner Dream number 11	They dream of casting the light of illumination; of being a true idealist. They secretly believe there is more to life than we can know or prove, and would like to be a provider of the 'word' from on high.

Why don't you look at the gifts numerology says you were born with? There are many websites which offer free numerology calculators.

See what your numbers say. See what you make of it. Soon we will look at these words to see if you can develop an idea of who you could be if these were your gifts, and what your lessons might be.

 Start now: Use the table below to record the results of your numerological Birth Gift.

Character number	
Soul number	
Inner dream	

What do you make of what you found above; do any of the words resonate with you? Do they feel right? Can you see how some words could describe you if this aspect wasn't blocked by something? An example of this would be a client who had the word 'energetic' but felt that having that level of energy was naughty and was told so growing up, so the energy had transformed. It was pushing to be recognised and came out as anxiety. Is there something in the words that you can see would do that for you? And lastly are there some words which you just do not recognise, they are just not you?

Use the following worksheet to identify which category the different words fit for you.

Words that fit	Words that could fit	Words that you don't recognise in yourself

Birth Cards

You may not realise that you have two or three tarot cards that correspond with your birth date. Your tarot birth cards are seen to represent your potential, qualities that will be helpful for you to develop, explore and balance throughout your life; qualities that shape your development.

There are a number of websites which will work out your birth cards. The one we use is by The Tarot School:

http://www.tarotschool.com/Calculator.html.

On this site you can also read an article by psychotherapist Dr Elinor Greenberg, who writes about how she uses the birth cards within her psychotherapy practice.

Once you have your cards, let your mind be free as you gently reflect on the pictures, allowing any thoughts or connections to arise.

You can draw or stick pictures of your Birth Cards here.

What did you find out? Take some time and reflect in your journal about how you feel about what you found. Remember though to stay on the Viewing Platform and not to become involved in the emotions. This isn't easy and if you do become emotional please take care of yourself and remember these are just Birth Gifts. You can do this with a friend, on your own or in conjunction with a therapist. The main thing is, whatever you choose, ensure you have a way of looking after yourself.

Now what we are going to do is to take the words you have just found and do the same with them as you did with your numerology. We're going to put them on a worksheet, identifying which ones fit you, which ones may fit and those that don't sound like you at all.

Words that fit	Words that could fit	Words that you don't recognise in yourself

Now things are starting to get interesting. What do you notice about the answers on this worksheet and the answers on the other worksheet?

Take some time comparing them; are they very similar or very different? How do you feel about what you have written? Plot them on the table on the next page so you can see how they appear.

Compare the two approaches on the worksheet.

Numerology			Birth Cards		
Words that fit	Words that could fit	Words that you don't recognise in yourself	Words that fit	Words that could fit	Words that you don't recognise in yourself

Astrology

The next area we look at is astrology and your star sign, to see what that gift says about you. You will be familiar with the system by now; we are going to do the same process for your astrology as we did for numerology and birth cards.

The first step is to identify your sun sign; you can use the chart below to help.

Sign	Birth date
Aries	March 21st - April 19th
Taurus	April 20th - May 20th
Gemini	May 21st - June 21st
Cancer	June 22nd - July 22nd
Leo	July 23rd - August 22nd
Virgo	August 23rd - September 22nd
Libra	September 23rd - October 23rd
Scorpio	October 24th - November 21st
Sagittarius	November 22nd - December 21st
Capricorn	December 22nd - January 19th
Aquarius	January 20th - February 18th
Pisces	February 19th - March 20th

Have a look at what you can find out about your astrology. Your sun sign is just a simple part of your astrological horoscope, giving a very generalised idea of characteristics. If this area interests you, you can take things further. There are free online generators of your personal horoscope, which will give you much more detail, or you can consult our own astrologer, Louise Edington, who offers special prices to any HTP clients.

Louise writes more about astrology and how it can be used in coaching, life purpose and counselling, in our book. She also contributes to our Facebook page. Louise's own page is:

https://www.facebook.com/YourCosmicBlueprint

Once you have identified your astrology sign, identify the key words associated with it and use the worksheet below to record them.

Words that fit	Words that could fit	Words that you don't recognise in yourself

Take some time out. Pause and consider what you know and how this has been for you; not just the information you are collecting but also on your journey of discovery. Are you finding new information? Is it interesting? Are you interesting? Ways to reflect could include what you are thinking and feeling and what you notice in your body. Is this work impacting on you; are you learning anything about you? Does this make sense to you? Reflect on the process of this and what (if anything) it brings up for you.

Try not to rush any of the life review exercises; take time, reflect, meditate, talk to people. There is no rush.

Would it be useful for you to talk to a friend now, a family member or a therapist about the fascinating person you are and what you are finding out and the impact it is having on you?

Chinese Horoscope

The next Birth Gift we look at is the Chinese horoscope and what animal is said to describe your personality. Below is a table, which shows you all the animals. Find your birth year and follow the table across to the animal. That is your Chinese astrology animal; for example if you were born in 1968, like me, you would be a monkey.

Rat	1912	1924	1936	1948	1960	1972	1984	1996	2008
Ox	1913	1925	1937	1949	1961	1973	1985	1997	2009
Tiger	1914	1926	1938	1950	1962	1974	1986	1998	2010
Rabbit	1915	1927	1939	1951	1963	1975	1987	1999	2011
Dragon	1916	1928	1940	1952	1964	1976	1988	2000	2012
Snake	1917	1929	1941	1953	1965	1977	1989	2001	2013
Horse	1918	1930	1942	1954	1966	1978	1990	2002	2014
Sheep	1919	1931	1943	1955	1967	1979	1991	2003	2015
Monkey	1920	1932	1944	1956	**1968**	1980	1992	2004	2016
Rooster	1921	1933	1945	1957	1969	1981	1993	2005	2017
Dog	1922	1934	1946	1958	1970	1982	1994	2006	2018
Pig	1923	1935	1947	1959	1971	1983	1995	2007	2019

You know the process by now; explore different websites and find out what your animal represents.

Then, as before, plot the results below.

Words that fit	Words that could fit	Words that you don't recognise in yourself

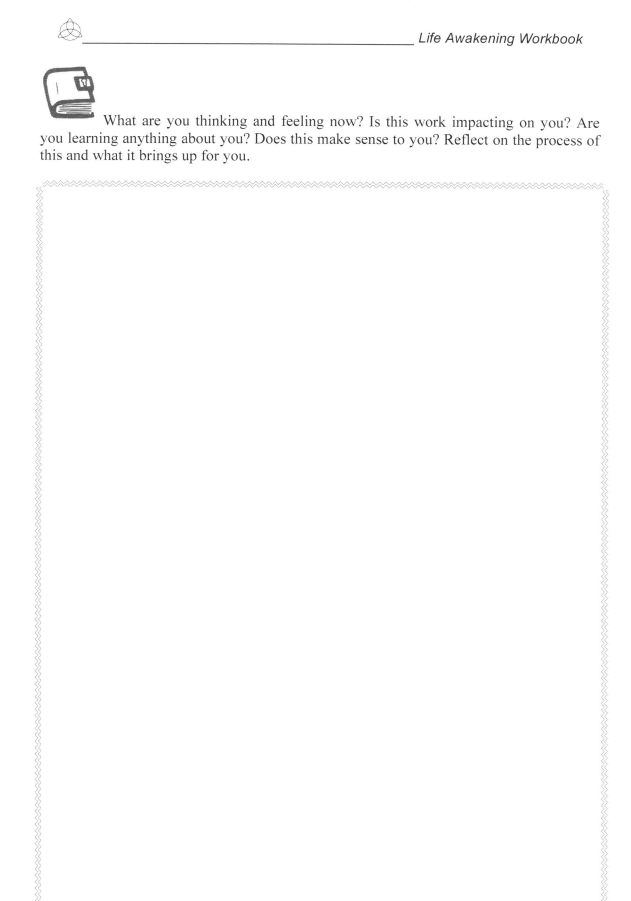

What are you thinking and feeling now? Is this work impacting on you? Are you learning anything about you? Does this make sense to you? Reflect on the process of this and what it brings up for you.

What we are going to do now is look at the words that do resonate with you, that make sense to you and the words that could fit, from all the three areas.

Write the words that resonate with you in this table.

Numerology	Birth Cards	Astrology	Chinese Astrology

Write the words that do not resonate with you in this table.

Numerology	Birth Cards	Astrology	Chinese Astrology

Game Time

This is the fun part. Stand on the Viewing Platform and detach yourself from feelings and judgements about the words and just look at them. You can do this bit alone or with your friends, your family, your therapist or anyone who wants to play the game.

The game is, who is this person and what would they be? Would you want to be friends with them? What career would you say they would go on to have? What information can you get from these Birth Gifts?

Jill says: I have included an example of Miriam's here so you can see what I mean. Allow your imagination to fly; there is no limit on what this baby can grow to be. It hasn't hit society yet, to tell it that it can't and instil it with fear, so the future is totally open; the only limit is your imagination.

Miriam's adjectives from this exercise reflected two distinct sides to her personality. She has a nurturing, motherly, caring, homemaking side, full of compassion and kindness; she knew this from her sun sign Cancer. Other adjectives that came out were about being radical, pioneering and taking up humanitarian causes.

When Miriam reflected on her life she could see that in her early adulthood her humanitarian, political side had dominated and then her profession as a therapist and becoming a mother had given precedence to her nurturing side. Miriam's best year recently was when she home educated her daughter for a year. At that time she felt really in balance with who she was, she had endless energy and enthusiasm, and running her therapy practice and a home school was busy, yet effortless.

In HTP we often take these times as signs when our energy or chi is flowing. When we work within our passion we can feel the difference. By reflecting on her adjectives Miriam realised that neither humanitarian causes nor nurturing, on their own, fully expressed her. When she was nurturing in a radical way, she felt balanced and whole.

When she was home schooling, she was nurturing but she was also being counter-cultural and passionate about the uniqueness and individuality of children. As she reflected on the adjectives that balance her, Miriam realised that the development of HTP could also offer her this balance and fulfilment, as its aim is to nurture and offer therapy in a way that is radical and values the uniqueness of each individual.

 Use this space to plot your ideas.

This baby can be anything; it is born with certain characteristics, which will aid it. What will it be? ……………

It's time to sit and reflect on what you have written and how this process was for you. Write in your journal what you experienced while imagining what this person would be.

Ensure you take care of yourself; this can be a difficult process and it's important to ensure you feel safe and secure whilst doing this. You may need to talk to your friends or family, see a therapist or join one of our HTP sessions, either individually or in a group. The most important thing is you and ensuring you're okay.

Now we are going to look at the words that didn't fit, which you couldn't see in yourself. Remind yourself what they are by writing them on the worksheet below.

Words that do not resonate

Numerology	Birth cards	Astrology	Chinese astrology

What do you make of these words? These may be as important as the ones you have identified with, because these may be part of your gifts. Don't dismiss them immediately. Are they ones that have not been allowed to develop; the ones you had but were told they are not useful, or ones you thought were not for you?

Reflect on what you think. Take your time, there is no rush to finish; the more depth of reflection and time given to this, the more you will get out of it.

Ancestors and Family

This section is for you to explore your family; who are they? What are the family stories? The information could be about the work your ancestors did, the relationships they had, and the things that were important to them. Some examples would be that my paternal grandfather worked as a stationmaster, an interesting job in itself, but it also enabled him not to have to go to war. Another would be my maternal grandmother, who had four husbands and outlived them all! Who in your family stands out? Who do people talk about and who are the quiet ones who never get mentioned?

Use your journal to write and reflect on your family stories. If it's possible you may want to ask other family members about any family stories.

What are your family stories and how do they make you feel? What do you think about them? Do any resonate with you?

Genogram

We will start with drawing your genogram: a genogram is a diagram that charts your family members and can be used across several generations.

The basic symbols used on a genogram are:

⬜ Male

⬭ Female

Jill says: To give you an idea I have included a genogram for my immediate family. I'm the white circle.

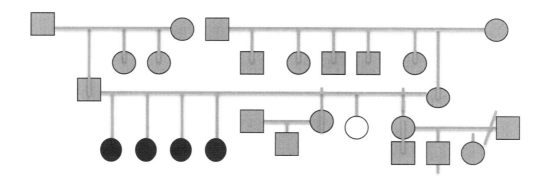

When I look at this what I see is that my father was the oldest child and the only boy, whilst my mother was the youngest of six. That makes me wonder about their relationship. The other thing I notice is the four miscarriages before me or my sisters were born. How would that impact on my family?

Draw your genogram. Don't worry if it's not perfect or there are things you don't know, that's normal. And you can use a different symbol on areas you don't know, because that could be interesting. Do as much as you can. I just did my immediate family to give you an idea, but if you know them, include grandparents, aunts, uncles etc.

Take time to reflect on what you have found. Some ideas for questions are:

What jumps out at you; are there any patterns?

What do you see in your family?

How do you think they impacted on you?

Would you choose to be born into this family?

What does this family give you, or not?

Take time; as with all the reflection exercises it takes time, there is no rush.

Parents

Parents are so influential on us for all our lives, whether they are here or not. If you ask someone about their parents, they have emotional reactions, whether they are happy memories or difficult parents, we remember or we are determined to forget, which is another story in itself.

So far we have been building up a picture of the family you were born into, recognising interesting aspects and any patterns. What we are going to do next is narrow down the information to just your parents. To explore who they are/were, what their purpose was in life, what characteristics you got from them and how they impacted on you.

This time we have a few questions to ask and for you to reflect on. Then there will be space for you to reflect and to add anything important which hasn't been asked.

Miriam's example

My father's purpose, as an academic, was to study in depth a key religious text, to find out the truth of what was being said. He learned ancient languages in order to read the text within its original language and he studied the history and context in order to understand the meaning. He felt very strongly that people should not misuse the Bible to support their own ill thought-through views.

My mother's purpose, as a nurse, was to support people as they gave birth and as they died. It was to find different and effective ways of easing pain and she also explored alternative medicines. She was interested in travel and missionary work when she was a young adult.

My purpose? I can see within me both my mother's desire to heal and to reach people and my father's desire to know and understand. I see my parents representing heart and head. Psychotherapy and developing HTP fits for me, in that my path appears to be a continuation of theirs.

Always remember to take care of yourself whilst working through these exercises; they may seem simple but they can elicit strong emotions, so self-care is paramount. If anything does arise from these exercises do speak to your friends or a therapist.

This exercise can be difficult especially if we can see the flaws and problems in the parenting we received, but we are trying to stay on the Viewing Platform and to see the higher intention and purpose of our parents, not to evaluate how well they achieved it!

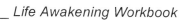

 Complete the following worksheet.

Parents exercise: father

Describe your father in three to five adjectives.

What would you say was his mission in life?

What would others say was his mission in life?

What would he say was his mission in life?

 Use your journal to reflect on both what you wrote above and how it felt to do it.

We are impacted by and learn so much from our parents, both positive and difficult. You have identified adjectives to describe them, how do you think someone with those characteristics can impact on a little baby?

Stand on the Viewing Platform and imagine you have a little baby and you are going to give it to the people with the characteristics described above to take care of. How does that make you feel?

What was the positive potential of these parents to look after and help this baby to grow? What do you think they would help the baby to learn; i.e. to be independent, to be free, to be family orientated, to be kind, to work hard, etc?

Take some time and let your imagination flow.

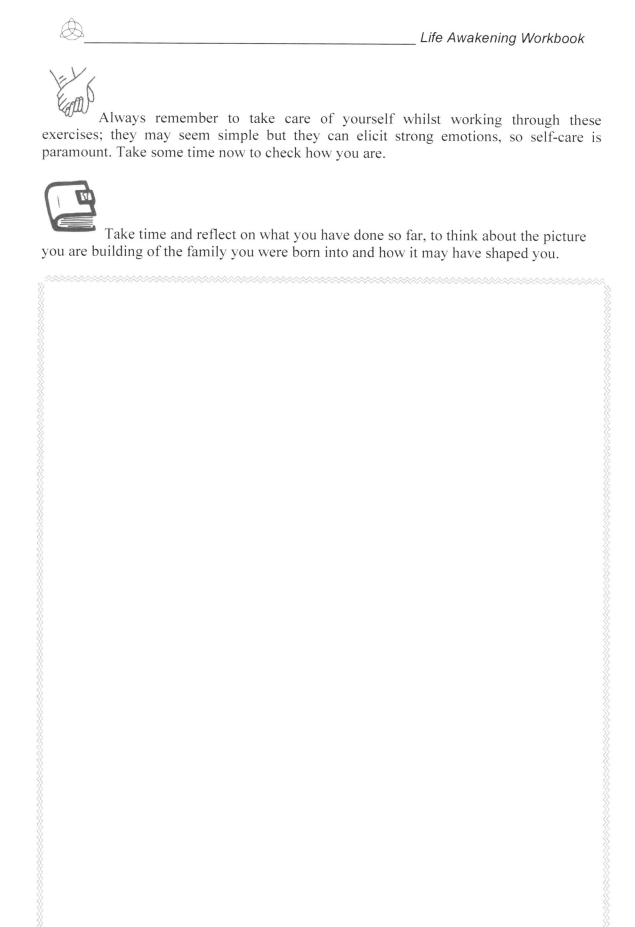

Always remember to take care of yourself whilst working through these exercises; they may seem simple but they can elicit strong emotions, so self-care is paramount. Take some time now to check how you are.

Take time and reflect on what you have done so far, to think about the picture you are building of the family you were born into and how it may have shaped you.

Remember to be kind to yourself as you remember yourself as a baby and to stay an observer on the Viewing Platform.

Take some time out now and think and write about what you found and how the experience was for you. Were there any surprises? Did it work? How do you feel about what you were told? Be creative and write whatever you like; it's your right whatever you feel you want to write.

Siblings and Birth Order

Were you an only child or did you have siblings? Being the eldest, youngest or middle child is part of the experience that shapes us too.

Sometimes one child gets more attention than the others, this may be because they are disabled or ill, or because they are seen as more important because of their gender. Some children are called 'accidents' (meaning they were not consciously planned), other children are born shortly after the cot death of a previous child. This would affect the child's psychology due to parent fear of attachment and loss, and it may also affect a child spiritually in terms of their deepest identity; they may feel a need to carry two personalities forward into life. What part might birth order have played with you?

  Reflect on and then write about these questions:

Were you an only child, eldest, youngest, middle, one of many?

Were you a twin?

Were there any lost or dead children?

Were you separated from siblings through adoption?

What was the gender balance within the siblings; one girl and five boys for example?

What were the responsibilities and role of the position you held in the family?

In relation to your siblings how were you supposed to be (eg, gentle to a sister, or caretaker for younger siblings, or quiet around a studious sibling)?

Do you feel birth order affected you?

You can research articles about the effects of birth order or being a twin if you feel this is an important area for you.

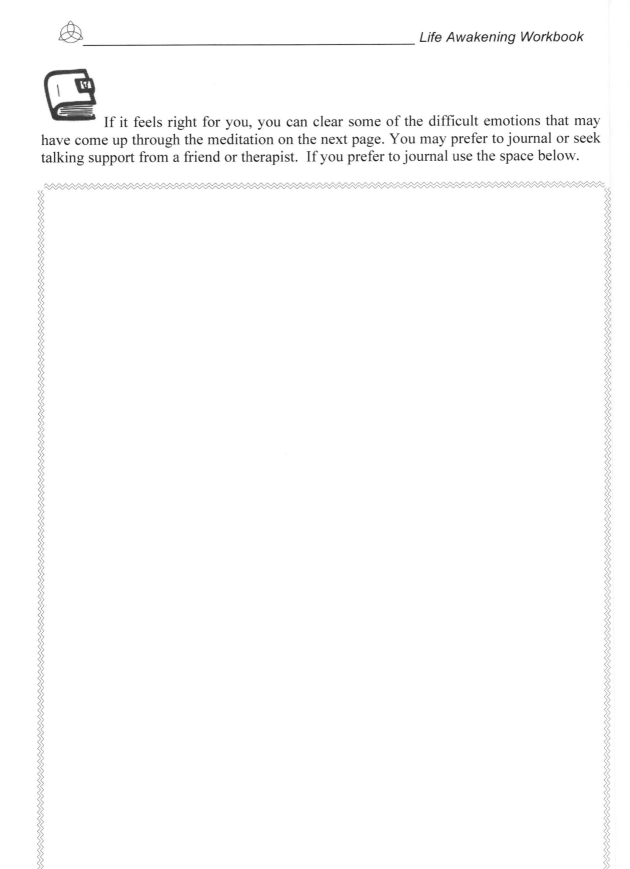

If it feels right for you, you can clear some of the difficult emotions that may have come up through the meditation on the next page. You may prefer to journal or seek talking support from a friend or therapist. If you prefer to journal use the space below.

Optional Healing Mediation

Close your eyes and prepare yourself as in the preparation exercise learned at the start of this course.

Breathe into your heart. Allow yourself to feel warmth and love within your heart. Imagine your heart glowing with pink light that expands a little with each breath.

Breathe in and feel the love in your heart expand until it fills your body and brings a smile to your face.

Let an image of yourself as a baby come into your mind and send this baby love.

Spend as long as you need, until you know that baby has received the love you have sent.

Smile and blow, or give, the baby you a kiss.

Place this image of yourself inside your heart, see the baby all nestled in. You can now blow the baby kisses anytime you want to.

Now let an image of each, or any, of your siblings, as a baby, come into your mind.

Allow yourself to see their goodness and potential as a baby (however they turned out to be later). See their true essence and highest potential, and send that baby love and peace.

Breathe gently and renew and restore your heart-love as necessary.

This may take time, you do not have to do this, but if you choose to do this, stay focused on the baby your brother or sister was.

When you have finished, you can place these babies in the huge universal heart, so they can be held there in love.

You can contribute to the universal heart energy, sending your brothers and sisters love, but you are not the sole heart for these babies to live within.

End the meditation by breathing cleansing breaths into your body and smiling.

Historical and Cultural Context

We are going to start this section by looking at your name.

Look up the meaning of your name and write it here.

What other meanings does your name have for you? For example, 'I was named after my uncle who was a war hero'.

We have looked at your family history and stories. We now go on to link these with the history and culture around us. We are curious as the creators of the Human Trinity Principles that we were born into a time when we could create this approach.

Miriam's example

My parents met on the boat travelling from Australia to Europe. The family history with both my parents being Australian is that there are clearly generations of people leaving home and family repeatedly. My parents settled as first generation immigrants within British society. In the time when they grew up, England was called 'home' although they had never been there! History and geography taught in their school were British history and geography!

Now we can see the cultural effect and the effect of history on the story we came to play a part in. My parents loved buying antiques before the time when antiques were valued. I spent a lot of my time going in the car to antique shops or house clearances because my parents wanted a lamp, old plates or a sideboard. In many ways they seemed to want more English and old English furniture than my friends' parents, who were wanting modern 70s TV units and crockery. Is this part of being not British? I often feel rootless without history, yet my parents were trying to buy history. I studied history in my spare time and at A level. Belonging and history has been a very important part of my personality.

Growing up in Sheffield during the miners' strike is also part of my culture. If I went to town, there were miners with buckets collecting money or tins of food. The City Council had an environmental policy whereby it was 2p to travel anywhere within Sheffield on the bus - the freedom to travel this gave us as children was fantastic. I grew up in a city of community and sharing, during a time of the entrepreneur and self-made businessman. I was also a teenager when we had the first female Prime Minister.

So I grew up privileged in the UK; white, female, educated, within a culture that increasingly listened to women and argued about treatment of others.

We will look at the history that happened around you more in part two of this course. For now let's look at the Birth Gifts of what you were born into.

Write five adjectives or find a picture online and stick it here, that represents the history and culture you were born into.

Take some time and reflect on what you wrote, the memories you had about those times and what they mean for you.

You are now going to explore in more depth the environmental factors around when you were born.

What country did you grow up in and in what decade/s were you most aware of the culture?

What were the significant political or historical events prior to your birth?

What is your family history relating to the world wars, if any?

What role did your family play in society and history (for example, were they gamekeepers or gentry, soldiers, shop keepers, pioneers)?

What values did this bring (for example, pride, frugality, deference, courage, invisibility)?

Consider if your parents brought other cultures and influences to the country of your birth and the impact.

Does your family have any story relating to prejudice due to race, class, and politics of the time?

What were the key concerns of the society you grew up in?

What does it mean to be 'British', 'Asian' etc (whichever identity you were born into)?

How would the history and culture around you when you were born teach you or challenge you?

Later on in part two we will look at unfolding political events after you were born.

Physical Gifts

Our bodies are a key part of the Trinity, and our DNA inheritance among other things is part of our experience. If you are born to have red hair, born female, born with the gene for irritable bowel, likely to be tall, are blind, have skinny legs, have a big nose; all these attributes, which are usually unalterable, have an impact on how we might get along in the world, whether we stand out or fit in, what types of illness we may be prone to and others' expectations of us.

Think about your gender, race, body type, gifts, illness, disability and strengths and list them here. Remember this is all about your potential; you are not supposed to be wondering why you didn't fulfil all your gifts, but simply noting what you had at the start; challenges and assets. Physical appearance has a big impact on people's lives, as do genetic pre-dispositions. Are you double-jointed? Did you inherit the need to wear glasses? Do you have freckles? Were you born with digits or limbs missing?

 Reflect on your physical gifts.

As well as the physical gifts you were born with there are also pre-birth and birth experiences as well. Consider the physicality of your womb and birth experience. What stresses, chemicals and experiences do you think you might have had before and during birth? Was your baby body strong or premature? Were you born easily or with difficulty? Did your life feel secure or in the balance? What chemicals did you receive in vitro due to stress, cortisol levels, nicotine, bereavement etc?

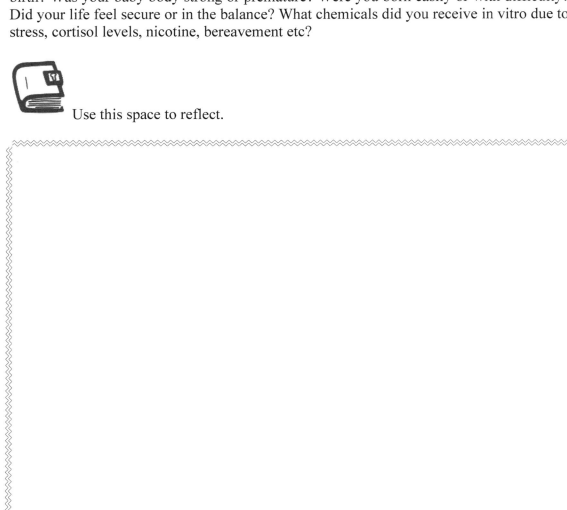 Use this space to reflect.

Well done, you have been on quite a journey and collated a lot of information.

Summary of Birth Gifts

Inner Voice - Reminder

In the preparation information, at the beginning of the workbook, there is a section on Inner Voice and how to access it. The Inner Voice is the true you, your true opinion based on you and your 'higher self'. It removes the obstacles and blocks to you being you, whether they are the messages learned as we grow up or beliefs we have about ourselves. We are born pure without negative thoughts; we learn these from society, what we should and shouldn't do and we take them on as truths. Your Inner Voice bypasses those beliefs and accesses the part of you that hasn't been touched by the world.

As with every new skill it takes time and practice to connect with your authentic self, so if it takes time don't worry. Your Inner Voice is always there but you may be out of practice listening to it. So ban any negative thoughts that may come if you don't do this perfectly the first time!! Use the worksheet below to write what you find out. Do write whatever you get, don't censor yourself or think, 'No that can't possibly be it.' There may be information you do not know yet and when you do it may become clearer. So just write everything.

Closing Meditation

Using your Inner Voice, meditate on your life purpose. Ask your Inner Voice for a symbol, picture, phrase or metaphor to take with you from this part of the workbook. Draw it here:

If you were to draft your life purpose now what would it be?

Journal Review

For the last journal entry for this section review all the journal entries you have made and the exercises you have undertaken and see what you find, what stands out for you, what strikes you as really interesting, and just as important the aspects which confuse you or are uninteresting; uninteresting things become interesting just by being uninteresting! Or they do to us anyway.

Conclusion

Well done, you have reached the end of this section of the workbook. You have identified a number of Birth Gifts and these are not all of them; you could spend a lifetime just exploring your Birth Gifts. We hope you do spend some time, not a lifetime; as we have said previously the more you explore the more you will find and the closer you will be to your life purpose.

We hope you have enjoyed exploring your Birth Gifts and the life you were born into. We now move on to what happened next; how did your Birth Gifts develop or not? So enjoy the next part of your journey.

PART TWO: FROM BIRTH GIFTS TO NOW; LIFE THEMES AND PATTERNS

Contents

The Triquetra Human Trinity Symbol

 Your Life In A Nutshell
   Your Mind-Body-Spiritual Journey so far
   Your Mind's Journey
   Your Body's Journey
   Your Spiritual Journey
 Your Life as a Fairy Tale
 Childhood Dreams
 Fantasies
 Childhood Stories About You
 Timeline
 Brief Overview of Your Life

Your Life in Relation to Your Birth Gifts

Conclusion to From Birth Gifts to Now

PART TWO
FROM BIRTH GIFTS TO NOW; LIFE THEMES AND PATTERNS

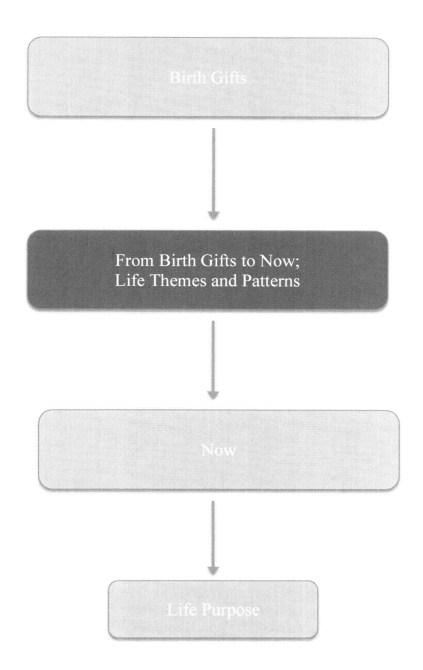

PART TWO

FROM BIRTH GIFTS TO NOW; LIFE THEMES AND PATTERNS

So far you have charted your unique Birth Gifts through seven different lenses and, we hope, wondered about what those Birth Gifts mean for you and reflected on your potential, from right back before life really got going.

In this section of the workbook you will look at how you can gain further clues from your life story and identify Life Patterns, through a further seven different activities and exercises. These clues will help you understand what you are drawn to and what lessons you keep enrolling in. The aim is by understanding the themes and patterns, you can gain insight into your final plan of action to wake up your life.

Again we were quite astonished to see, in our experience of charting our first HTP seekers, and ourselves, that there was a clear correlation between Birth Gifts and childhood patterns. So suspend judgment, let's get back up onto that Viewing Platform and watch your life unfold!

This section can be quite emotional, so remember the important guidelines at the front of this guide regarding preparation and support. The workbook is designed to ensure you only go as deep as is comfortable for you. As with physical exercise, if it hurts, stop doing it. Remember this is a review from a Viewing Platform. It is not therapy (that might come later for you if necessary). For now we are looking to see what areas stand out for you as needing attention or what areas point you towards finding your unique 'make and model'.

The Triquetra Human Trinity Symbol

The Human Trinity Principles work with the triquetra symbol and the idea that we are made up of a trinity of Mind-Body-Spirit. In order to conduct a complete Life Review or plan a holistic therapy, or any wholly-rounded action plan, we look at ourselves as a human trinity.

The word triquetra is Latin for three-cornered. The Celtic triquetra below is constructed with three interlocked circles. As with many Celtic intertwined lines, there is no beginning and no end, representing eternity, and indicating for us the flow and movement in HTP. The triquetra has been used historically as a religious symbol of things and persons that are threefold.

The triquetra is a Celtic knot. Knotwork patterns are symbolic of life's journey, spiritual quest and an attempt to make sense of the maze of existence.

They represent a continuity of life with no beginning and no end, a journey to one's spiritual centre, an inner quest for spiritual rebirth, and a pathway to the sacred and divine source.

Meditate upon the symbol. Let your imagination soar when contemplating the Celtic knotwork or symbolism. Your personal interpretation will ultimately be your best guide, and the only answer you need. Note down any connections you made or draw any symbols that occurred to you.

It has been quite a journey from your birth until today, so what we are going to do to start, is to have a brief look at the overall pattern of your life. Complete the worksheet on the next page.

Your Life in a Nutshell

To complete this worksheet start on your Viewing Platform, then for each year write one or two memories, just a few words which will help you remember. It could be the name of your school, the street you lived on, the name of a friend, a place you visited that year, any word which is linked to a memory. The worksheet starts at birth but few people remember much from the early years so do not worry if you do not have any memories for the first few years, do what you can. Continue on a separate sheet if required.

Year	Word or two for a memory	Year	Word or two for a memory
0		36	
1		37	
2		38	
3		39	
4		40	
5		41	
6		42	
7		43	
8		44	
9		45	
10		46	
11		47	
12		48	
13		49	
14		50	
15		51	
16		52	
17		53	
18		54	
19		55	
20		56	
21		57	
22		58	
23		59	
24		60	
25		61	
26		62	
27		63	
28		64	
29		65	
30		66	
31		67	
32		68	
33		69	
34		70	
35		71	

   Take time now and reflect on what you have written; that's your life, that's how your life has unfolded so far. This is one of those exercises in which you can reflect on a very basic level, for example just noticing the patterns in the words chosen. The first time I did it I was quite amused to find I had written lots of places. The first time Miriam did it she had lots of names, she's obviously a people person! I wondered what that said about the way we remember our lives? So that's quite simplistic and you can look at it in more depth and look for deeper patterns of relationships, patterns of employment, patterns of development.

One thing to note, especially if you have been through difficult times, is that they pass or end. When you run through your life and remember different aspects, remember they may have ended now. Sometimes it can be helpful to remember 'this too will pass'.

Use the page below to reflect on what you have written.

Your Mind-Body-Spiritual Journey so Far

Your Mind's Journey

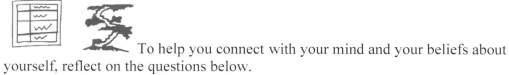 To help you connect with your mind and your beliefs about yourself, reflect on the questions below.

If you were to describe yourself growing up what would you say? A good child, a naughty, mischievous child? Energetic, studious, fantasist?

Do you know what beliefs you have about yourself today? Can you plot where they came from?

Can you remember thinking about yourself as a child and thinking what type of child you were?

Take some time to reflect on your mind's journey so far; can you see how your beliefs about yourself have developed? How was it for you looking at your thinking? Can you see how your child's brain worked? Can you see your uniqueness?

Miriam says: I see this as if we are running on old software; it works, but it isn't the most efficient or useful for our current life. This course aims to help you identify old software so you can upgrade.

Your Body's Journey

To help you connect with your body's journey, ask yourself the following questions. Do this from the Viewing Platform; at the moment we are gathering information rather than becoming involved in the emotions connected with your life story. Although if you do become involved in any emotions, write them down and let yourself know you will return to them later.

Remember the Birth Gifts of your body and the story of your birth. Travel your life line and look at your body's story. You may want to reflect on the following questions:

Were you breast or bottle-fed?
Were you fed on demand or by the clock?
Were you sickly?
Do you think you were warm and sheltered?
Did you have any baby illnesses? Or immunisations or accidents?

What attitudes to eating and feeding did you pick up?
Did your carers want you to not be messy, finish all you were given, not get fat, like all they cooked? Did they make good food choices for you?
Did you feel you could control your eating or that others did?

Do you remember your toilet training?
Did you find it easy or hard to control your body in this area?

Did you have any accidents as a child?
Did you suffer any other traumas?

How did you approach adolescence and the physical changes there?
Did you feel afraid, ashamed, supported, proud?
How did you choose to dress yourself or wear your hair? Were these your choices?
Was it possible in your family to express yourself through your body?

What have you put into your body choicefully: foods, drugs, contraception, cigarettes, alcohol?

What sexual experiences have you had; were these positive?
What experiences of exercise, dance, adventure has your body had?

Have you experienced pregnancy, infertility, childbirth, termination or miscarriage?
What was the impact?
Did you feel supported, ashamed, afraid?
What medical interventions have you had and how did this impact?

Have you experienced loss of parts of your body?
How well has your body been treated in your life?
How healthy has your body been through your life?

Consider if you need some support, to talk to a friend, or a therapist, or get a hug from someone. The Viewing Platform allows us to see that many people's lives are peppered with bodily experiences which are often shrouded in secrecy or shame.

To let go of unnecessary guilt or shame you may want to talk through the difference between taking responsibility and taking blame. This will be covered further in the workshops and main book in more depth.

Take some time to reflect on your body's journey so far; it's been quite a life, and you may never have linked all this information together, so be gentle with yourself.

Thinking it over, how much has body awareness featured in your life? How much have you noticed your body's story in your life? What do you conclude from this and notice? How was this process for you?

Your Spiritual Journey

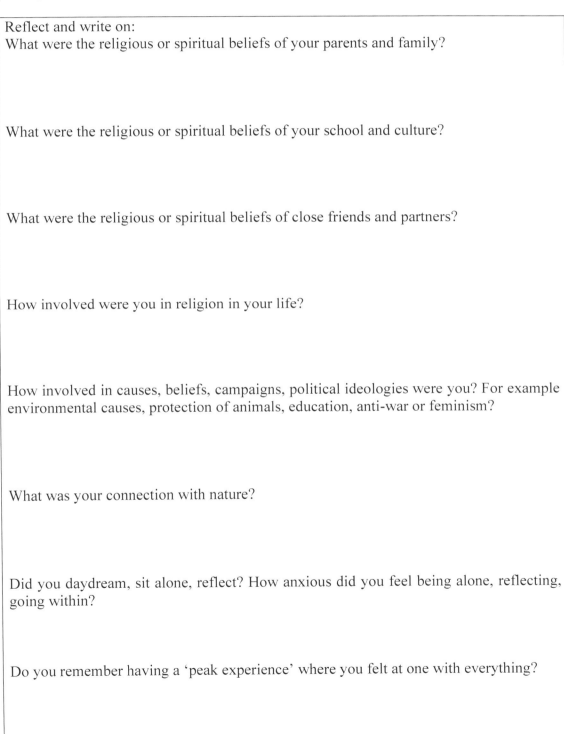

Spirituality may or may not have featured strongly in your development. Reflect on the following questions to help you remember your spiritual journey.

Reflect and write on:
What were the religious or spiritual beliefs of your parents and family?

What were the religious or spiritual beliefs of your school and culture?

What were the religious or spiritual beliefs of close friends and partners?

How involved were you in religion in your life?

How involved in causes, beliefs, campaigns, political ideologies were you? For example environmental causes, protection of animals, education, anti-war or feminism?

What was your connection with nature?

Did you daydream, sit alone, reflect? How anxious did you feel being alone, reflecting, going within?

Do you remember having a 'peak experience' where you felt at one with everything?

What did you learn or conclude from this? Use the space below to reflect.

Your Life as a Fairy Tale

 On these next few pages turn your life story into a fairy tale; you are the central character and everyone else plays a part in your fairy tale. So are you Cinderella, Hansel & Gretel, Little Red Riding Hood? Or a completely new character?

Let your imagination run wild. Enjoy!

Did you enjoy that? Did it come easily? What do you make of what you wrote?

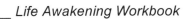

 Write about your experience of doing this in the box below.

You have plotted, and reflected on, an overview of your life from birth until now. What we will do next is to take you through your life in more depth, to pick out significant events and explore them further.

Childhood Dreams

This section includes a meditation. The aim is to encourage you to relax and allow the memories to flow. Remember to do this from the Viewing Platform and not to get involved with the emotions; it's just like watching a television programme.

So are you ready for a journey into your childhood?

> _Take a journey into the past:_
> _Find a comfortable place to sit or lie down, with no distractions. Gently breathe and notice the breath arriving and departing and arriving again in its own natural rhythm and waves. If you have meditation music, you can play it in the background._
>
> _With each out breath, let the tension release._
> _Release from your head, your eyes, your mouth and jaw, your scalp and ears._
>
> _Let your neck become free, your shoulders become wide and open, your arms release and your fingers relax._
>
> _Breathe into your rib cage; front, back and sides._
> _Release your pelvis, think of it as giving you a big open smile._
>
> _Relax and release your thighs, your knees, your calves and let all the tension drain out of your feet and toes._
>
> _Bring your attention to your centre, your middle. Notice how you can always return here when your mind wanders._
>
> _Now let yourself be in your safe space. Picture and imagine this safe space._
>
> _Now it is time to climb up onto your Viewing Platform . Remember you may like to be there alone or you may like a companion with you; a safe person, an animal, an angel or a guide. At all times remember you are watching this from your Viewing Platform and you can return to your safe place at any time._
>
> _Looking out from your platform, you see once again the baby we discovered in our Birth Gifts work. Now watch that baby grow into a bigger baby. Then a toddler._
>
> _Watch that child playing, thinking, growing and talking. What does the child like and not like? What does s/he do? Who is around her / him?_
>
> _Watch the child go to school and learn._
> _What stands out most from viewing childhood? Notice and move on._
>
> _Now the child is a teenager, and may take exams. What is happening in this teenager's life? How is he or she doing?_
>
> _Stop at about 14 years old._
> _Don't spend a long time, just observe from the platform and get a flavour._

Remember to care for yourself, to ensure you have support while you work through this workbook. Some people may not feel anything whilst others will. Both are fine.

Take some time and write some of your memories in your journal. Write how you feel about them now as an adult.

Can you see how this has aided or blocked the development of your Birth Gifts? To give you an idea, one of our clients talked about being told she was naughty when she was energetic. This taught her that being energetic is naughty and she pushed that down until it erupted in anxiety. Once she learned that being energetic was okay, she felt a release and managed to overcome many of her anxieties.

Fantasies

You have reflected from the Viewing Platform on your observations of growing up. Now we invite you to remember your childhood dreams, to get involved in those memories and emotions. What did you want to be when you grew up? An artist, a vet, an astronaut, superman, wonder woman, a banker? Do you remember? Do you remember the feeling of wanting to be something? How did you act on it as a child? Do you remember the games you played?

Jill's example

To give you an idea, I wanted to be a television character called Quincy. Quincy was a pathologist, but the exciting part was not just how people died, but who killed them? People fascinated me, as did the problem of how they work both physically and emotionally, although at that age I can't say I was sophisticated enough to explain it that way. So what did I do? I read books and I played at being a spy, to watch and follow the clues, to catch the killer.

Did I become a pathologist or a detective? No. However as a cognitive behavioural psychotherapist, I embraced the idea of problem solving with people; what's the problem, how do we understand it, how do we overcome it? And isn't it interesting that I then incorporated more relationally-based approaches, and then extended my interest to the body? Death could be called a spiritual event, so I can see how my interest as a child has led me to where I am today.

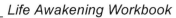 Use this space to write about what you wanted to be and how that has developed.

Childhood Stories about You

You have had an overview of your life and now started to explore more about the details in your childhood. You have written about your dreams and fantasies, now remember and write about the childhood stories you have about you. What are other people's memories of you and how you were? You may know some stories and you may want to ask your family, and friends you grew up with, if they know any more.

Miriam's example

A favourite story of my family about me takes place when I was age four. I was told to go to bed while the adults continued to talk downstairs. My father tells me that I stamped my feet, banged the door frame with my fist and asserted with frustration, 'But I want to know what pre-destination means! NOW!' For me this little picture frame captures an essential part of my continuing personality: I want to be included, I am intrigued and compelled to know, to explore with others, to learn and understand. I want to grasp the greater concepts of the universe and I most definitely don't want to stop mid-exploration, I want to know NOW!

 Use this space to write about your childhood stories.

How was remembering and writing that for you?
Easy? Difficult? Funny? Emotional?

Timeline

A timeline is always useful to plot significant events in our lives, to start to identify the impact they have on us.

Use this timeline to identify significant events in the first 14 years of your life.

Birth

14 years

Take care when doing this exercise. Ensure you have enough support and if it becomes too difficult, stop and take a break.

As you know, we are interested in mind, body and spirit and how they have developed or been blocked. To help you identify your development and blocks we have included three timelines, one for each. They are squiggly lines as we don't think life is that straight a line. You may not have much in this section or you may have more on one line than another, that's normal.

Jill says: To give you an idea, what I could include would be being told my sister is more intelligent, so I'm stupid. That would go in the mind section. In the body section I could note I was overweight, I had my tonsils out and fell off a wall. In the spirit section I could note the age I was when I went to Sunday school.

Miriam says: I remember being about 12 years old when I wondered about why I was me and not someone else, which could be perceived as spiritual. Also my frustration with 'what is outside the universe' lost me sleep from a young age.

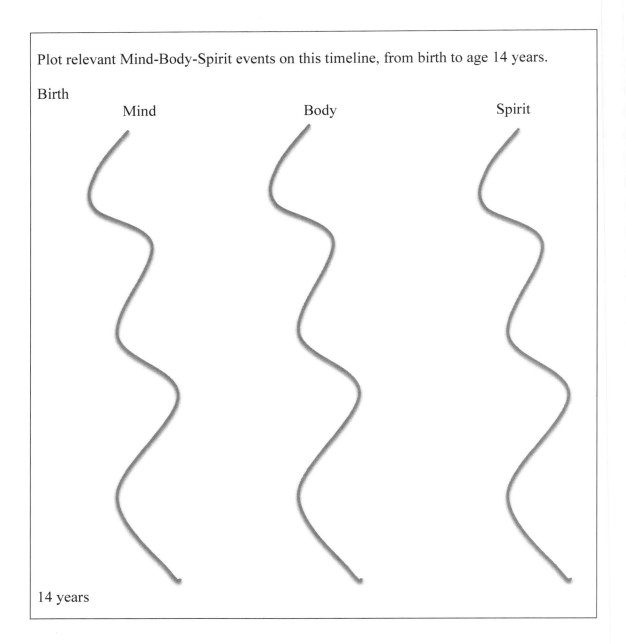

Plot relevant Mind-Body-Spirit events on this timeline, from birth to age 14 years.

Birth

Mind   Body   Spirit

14 years

Use the page below to reflect on what you have written. Did you remember anything new? How was it for you to look at the significant events in your early childhood? Did you notice anything interesting?

Jill says: While writing it, I thought about my sister, so I could reflect on that and the comparisons my parents made between us. Did it impact on me? Did it impact on my relationship with my sister? Is it why I haven't left school yet?

How do you think your early years impacted on you? Do they still impact?

Are you starting to get a picture of what you were like as a child, as well as what happened to you? It's important to notice the way you respond to significant events, so you can see how you grow as a person. The early years are when your individuality starts to show and grow. Are you starting to see <u>you</u>?

You were, and are, a unique human being; no one else is quite like you. We only need to look out at the world to see people are unique with different interests and ways of being. That is fantastic as it makes you individual and all the jobs are done! If we were all the same and all wanted to be firefighters there wouldn't be any teachers, bankers, domestic goddesses, etc. We may share characteristics, but we are all unique. Are you finding your uniqueness?

In case you are struggling to see who you were, answer the following questions.

When I was a child I wanted to be…

When I was a child I always loved to…

My childhood superhero / favourite fictional character was…

Childhood illnesses and accidents came at times when around me …

My greatest childhood achievements were in these areas…

I was happiest when…

I learned to cope by…

So now you have an idea of what was emerging as you grew up, and you may have already noticed some blocks. For example, you may have wanted to be a pilot but your parents wanted you to be a doctor so you did that instead. Or maybe you were in a family which didn't have an academic background so couldn't see the importance of school. Maybe that stopped you going forward with education.

Let's see what happened next on your journey to becoming you.

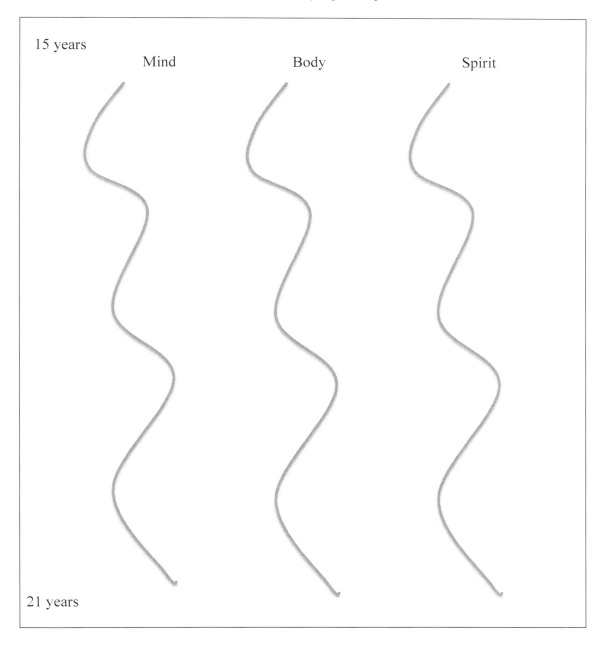

Undertake the same process for the years 15-21. They are also important years in your life, the years when you are finding out more about who you are.

This time put significant events and Mind-Body-Spirit aspects on the same worksheet.

Use the sheet below to write about how you feel about your life between 15 and 21 years. Can you be compassionate to the young you, growing up with the growing pains of adolescence and the mistakes we all make then? Be gentle with yourself and remember how young you were and how at that age people rarely know better, even if their parents say they should!

How was it being you? How was it revisiting you? What type of adolescent were you: studious, wild, in love?

We will follow the same process for the rest of your life, so in this section do your timeline for 22 – 28 years.

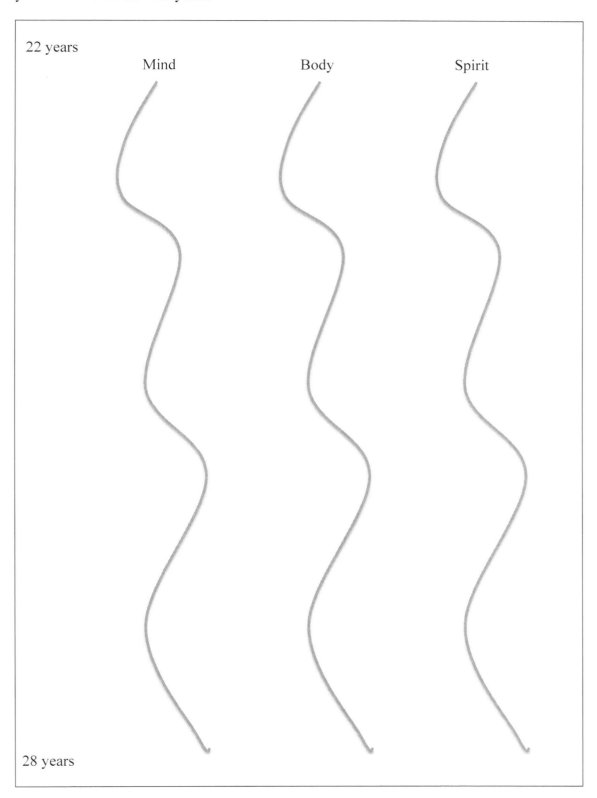

Write in the sheet below how this stage of your life was for you. Did you become what you set out to become? Do you still hold those childhood dreams or had they got lost by now? When did you lose your dream, or if you found your dream how was that for you?

What, if anything, blocked your progress? Was it circumstances, your beliefs about yourself, an ailment?

Can you see how you are growing to be an adult, becoming more of you, maybe even starting a family of your own? What type of relationships did you have, if any?

We move further along your life and see what happened next, what happened between 29 and 42 years old.

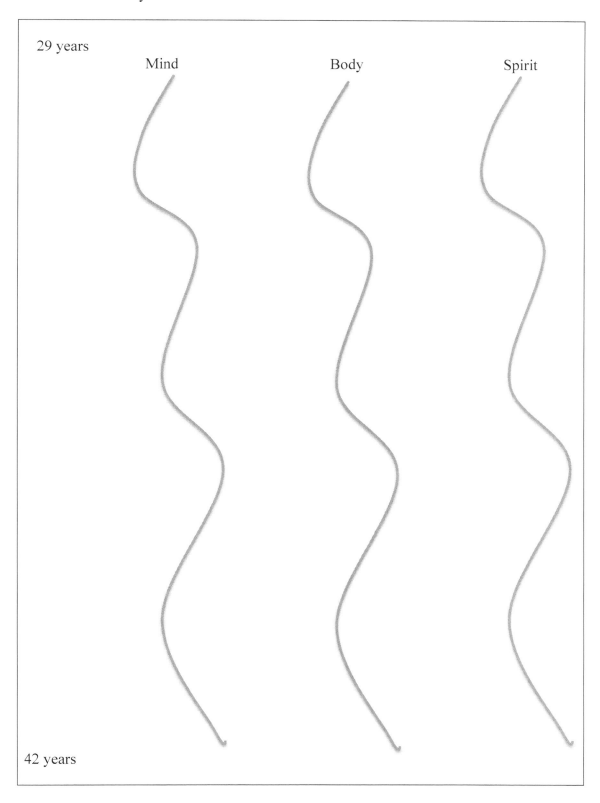

How was this period of time for you? How was it reviewing this period? Are you noticing how you feel while you review your life? How is it for you to remember: to remember the joys, the tears, the endings, the beginnings? Was this a happy time or a more difficult time? Can you see if your belief systems were activated much at that time of your life? Were you energised and enjoying life or had you lost your energy?

This time we will do from 43 years old to your current age. Plot the significant or most meaningful events below.

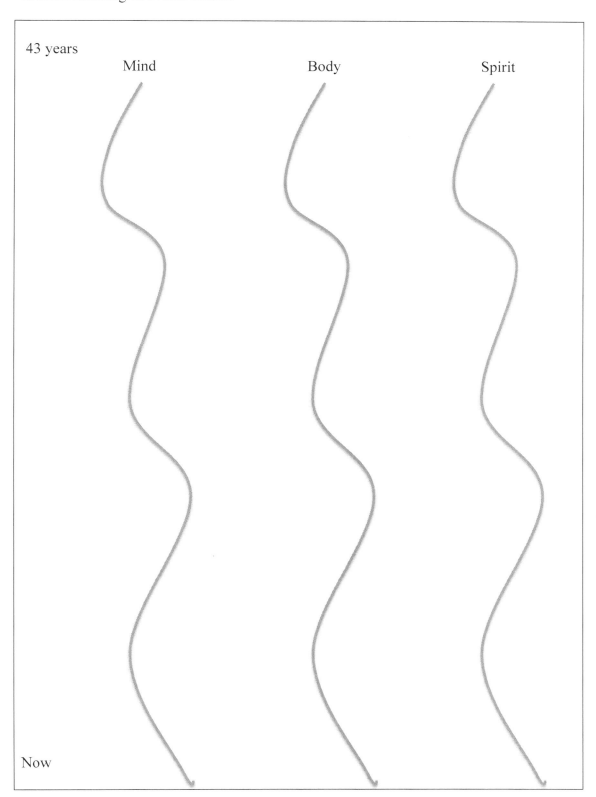

Use the sheet below to follow the previous process. Write about what you have found and how going through the process made you feel. What impact, if any, did it have on you? Are you noticing biases towards developing your mind, your body or your spirit? Are you replaying old patterns of behaviour, old patterns of relationships?

Brief Overview of Your Life

To end this part let's have a brief overview of your life. Here are a few reflective points to ask yourself.

My jobs have been….   and are linked in these ways …

My romantic partners were similar and different in these ways …

I was happiest in my jobs and relationships when…

I have lived in these places and feel …

My changing identities were …   and happened easily / with difficulty…

I kept being drawn to…

The key themes / repeating themes over the decades of my life are…

Every Person's Life is Worth a Novel

Sometimes it is helpful to think what sort of a novel our life would be, or what sort of a play or film. Is it a tragedy, a comedy, a trilogy, a magical play or story?

The reason it is important to understand what sort of story we are writing is that it will help us to get the final scene we want. Think of it this way, if every scene in your life story is written as if it were a Thomas Hardy novel, there is no way you are going to get a happy ending! And so if we think about the sort of novel you want your life to be, the moral of the story, the genre of the story, we can now begin to plant the seeds within today's chapter or today's scene.

So begin to think of yourself as the hero or heroine within the novel of your life. What genre would you choose if you started to write today? What trials or tribulations would befall you and would you overcome them and how? What is the moral of your story, the conclusion? What is your final message?

This is important because whether we are conscious of it or not we are writing the story. We have been writing this story for many years, usually unconsciously.

The trouble with *unconscious* writing of the story is that it will feel as if our life happens to us. If we can choose our story now, if we can write the scenes in the chapters consciously, we can direct the dream, we can direct the tale.

In the Human Trinity Principles, waking up to the dream of our life, writing our script, writing our novel, or writing our story, is a key part of *choosing* our life path.

Use this space to write the novel, play, film or poem that is your life so far.

Did you enjoy doing that? Was it easy? Did it start to flow once you started or was this actually a difficult process for you?

Your Life in Relation to your Birth Gifts

Use this sheet to reflect on the overview of Birth Gifts from section one and what you have found in this section. Can you see how the child has developed with the gifts they were born with or how the gifts have been blocked? What thoughts do you have regarding your life and how it has developed? Link it back to your Birth Gifts and the job you gave that little baby in the first section of this book.

Consider if you need some support, to talk to a friend or a therapist, or get a hug from someone.

Closing Exercise

 Meditate upon this Celtic trinity symbol and reflect on your own Trinity.

Which areas, Mind-Body-Spirit, were supported to grow in your life?

Which areas, Mind-Body-Spirit, suffered or struggled?

How would this fit your Birth Gifts? How did your childhood and adulthood reflect your Birth Gifts, both esoteric and family-given?

Do the patterns and themes make sense in light of your Birth Gifts? If your life was a novel or a play, do the opening scenes make sense of what follows?

 Write about your experience of the meditation.

 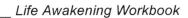

How would you like the story to continue and progress, from now on into the future?

Conclusion to Part Two

Well done, you have reached the end of this section of the workbook. You have reviewed and reflected on the journey of your life. We hope you do spend more time exploring your life; as we have said previously the more you explore the more you will find and the closer you will be to your life purpose.

We hope you have enjoyed exploring your journey. We now move on to Now and how your life is today.

PART THREE: NOW
Contents

Archetypes and the Human Trinity Principles
    List of Archetypes and Meanings
    Sub-personalities
    Continuing our Archetype Work

Presentation

Psychological Now:
    Seeker's own Description
    Myers Briggs
    Enneagram
    Beliefs and Introjects
    Environmental stressors

Physical Now:
    Seeker's own Description
    Physical Assessment of Body Input and Output
    Movement and the Self
    Chinese Five-Elements
    Body Care

Spiritual Now:
    Seeker's own Description
    Chakras
    Dream and Intuit your Destiny

Conclusion to Part Three

Your Life Review - What to do Next

PART THREE
NOW

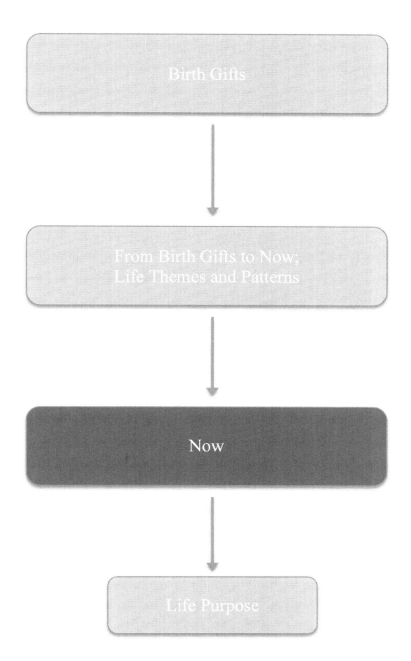

PART THREE

NOW

We are on a journey to discover and enjoy your own uniqueness. When we fully know who we are we will find life flows more easily, we will have more energy, and feel happier. An apple tree can't grow pears, a dolphin doesn't climb trees. Imagine if we really knew our 'make and model', how easy life would be?

Now section is a review of where you are now. At the end of this section we will move on to look at what to do with the work we have done, the journey and the discoveries we have made. The sneak preview to this secret is the Paradoxical Theory of Change. That is that simply by being ourselves we will achieve all we need to live happy and fulfilled lives. In order to be ourselves we are currently looking at who we are from all angles. Archetype work is a principle way of doing this. we see it like a photo-fit, 'I'm a bit like this, but not that part, and a bit like this too.'

We come to look at ourselves in the Now. This section would be familiar to any practitioner or client who goes for psychological or physical therapy. As we are working with the Human Trinity Principles, this assessment goes further, we will be making a Now assessment in *three* areas, using the HTP triquetra model.

Using classic psychological terms, a current physical analysis and energy assessment we will work to bring these pieces of information together within the Human Trinity Principles triquetra, to look at learning so far, to re-discover our unique balance in line with our own 'make and model', and to find what our Inner Voice leads us to do next.

The Inner Voice work you have been developing so far will help you to feel confident in dousing within the 'world wide web' of healing information that is out there, if we are willing to use our intuition and Inner Voice. There is much more on 'dousing the world wide web' of healing, the three wells of well-being and using intuition and Inner Voice, within our main book and key text, showing how we use these concepts and methods within the HTP model.

There is also more in our book about why we keep returning to the idea of life purpose and being on our path. Our research has led us to believe this is crucial to well-being and health. Thus this whole course is leading us to the final box in the flow chart: Life Purpose.

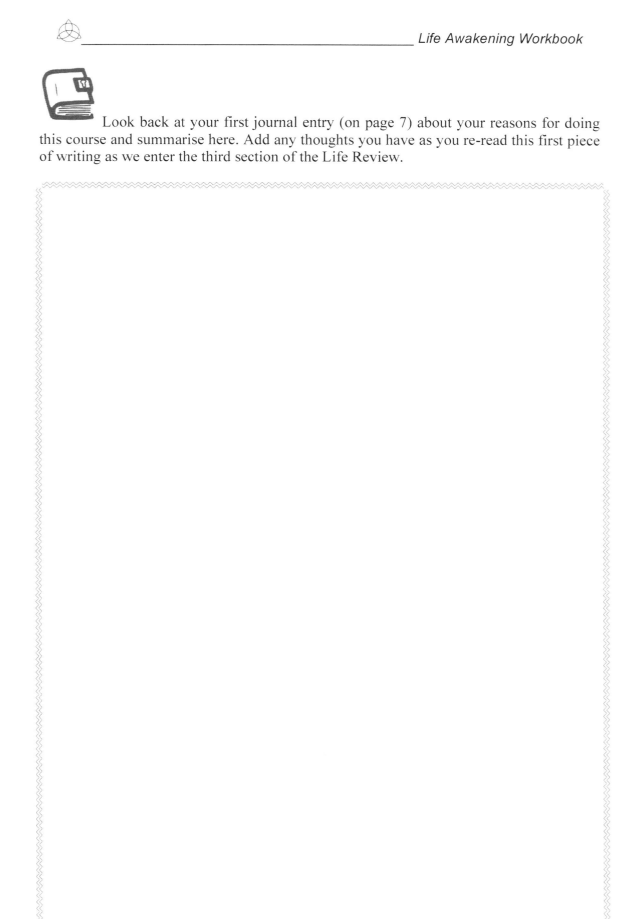

Look back at your first journal entry (on page 7) about your reasons for doing this course and summarise here. Add any thoughts you have as you re-read this first piece of writing as we enter the third section of the Life Review.

Archetypes and the Human Trinity Principles

What are archetypes and why do we use them? Archetypes are essentially a caricature, classic archetypes might be gods and goddesses, there are Jungian archetypes, mythical archetypes and modern archetypes.

Let's have a look at some characters and archetypes. Earth Mother is an archetype, Saboteur or Victim are other classic archetypes. Modern archetypes might be Superman, Gandalf, Zelda or Spock.

In our work to discover our uniqueness we have been looking at what we are similar to in general terms and this is what pre-psychoanalytic traditions used. For instance in tarot there are four elements: earth, air, fire and water. Air is associated with intellect, knowledge and the trials in life, water with emotions, intuition and love, fire with home, drive, innovation and creativity and earth with material aspects, wealth and abundance.

List of Archetypes and Meanings

Caroline Myss is a key writer on archetypes and has her own structure as how to undertake archetype work.

http://www.myss.com/library/contracts/determine.asp

> ***Caroline Myss in her book Sacred Contracts (2001) says:***
> Some of the archetypes in the list will jump out at you as if to say, 'You know me! I've been part of your life ever since you can remember.' It could be an archetype that is aligned with your occupation - for example, the Politician, Craftsperson, Athlete, Teacher, Scholar, or Judge. It might also be an important characteristic that defines your nature apart from your work, as the Monk or Nun (assuming you're not actually under holy orders), the Poet, Lover, Rebel, and so forth. But then you will have to dig a little deeper. Some archetypes that you may feel drawn to, like the Mystic, Visionary, or Healer, may be largely a matter of wishful thinking. Many of my students like to see themselves as Mystics, for instance. But I ask them to take a serious look within and determine whether the hard work and sacrifice that go with that identity have been a part of their life for many years. Some people like to be mystics during their summer retreat, or on the weekend, or for half an hour every morning, and that's great. But to include an archetype in your intimate family of 12, you need to be able to trace its life-long influence on you.

We ask you to read Caroline Myss's approach to archetypes and to use your Inner Voice to decide how you want to use this perspective. The HTP approach is simply to explore where your Inner Voice leads and then to dialogue with yourself and sub-personalities as appropriate.

After meditating with your Inner Voice, take four different-coloured pens and move through the list of archetypes (there are many more) and ask your Inner Voice to direct you. Circle in one colour those archetypes you can relate to, use a different colour for those you can't relate to and a third colour to circle those you feel ambivalent about. The fourth coloured pen is to add any other archetypes that come to your mind as you meditate.

Actor	Addict	Alchemist	Anarchist	Artist	Avenger
Beggar	Bully	Bureaucrat	Caregiver	Child	Clown
Companion	Coward	Craftsperson	Crone	Crook	Damsel
Detective	Dictator	Dilettante	Diplomat	Disciple	Diva
Dreamer	Evangelist	Fool	Gambler	God	Goddess
Gossip	Healer	Hermit	Historian	Innovator	Judge
Knight	Liberator	Lover	Magician	Martyr	Masochist
Matriarch	Midas	Monk	Muse	Mystic	Networker
Nun	Olympian	Patriarch	Pilgrim	Pioneer	Poet
Politician	Predator	Priest	Prince	Princess	Prophet
Prostitute	Provocateur	Puck	Puppet	Puritan	Rebel
Redeemer	Rescuer	Revolutionary	Robot	Saboteur	Sadist
Sage	Samaritan	Scholar	Scribe	Scout	Seductress
Seeker	Seer	Servant	Settler	Shaman	Sidekick
Slave	Spoiler	Storyteller	Student	Teacher	Thief
Tramp	Trickster	Tyrant	Vampire	Victim	Visionary
Warrior	Witch	Wizard	Zombie		

Sub-personalities

We can imagine we have several personalities within us. In psychosynthesis it is understood that our own unique sub-personalities make up our individuality. They can also steer the true self off track. For example, the true self might be steering a direction of self-enlightenment and peace, and the Glutton or the Teenager within us may sabotage this, as we wake up and log onto facebook instead of doing meditative practice. We have further in-depth information, exploration and examples of sub-personality work in our key text, *Life Awakening*.

Miriam's example

This is probably my favourite psychosynthesis work in terms of working with internal conflict or stuckness. I have a cast list, a few of these I am willing to share. Each of these came to me in meditation and their names are not always archetypal names but names that come to me:

Mother, Wise Woman, The Professor, Little Mim, Mermaid, Tree, Caretaker, Bus Driver.

Through meditation I discovered The Professor is a head with no body (so he thinks) and doesn't eat or care for himself (this is an aspect of me). Through dialogue I also have Mother, who once I had discussed it with her, agreed to take The Professor on so that she can make sure I am fed while I write this workbook!

My Caretaker reminds me of Filch from the Harry Potter books, a very 'jobs-worth' obsessive who does his job and is not capable of seeing the larger picture of what is important, or bending the rules. Without my Caretaker I wouldn't get some essential tasks done, but if he ruled the roost, I know I would alienate people around me, I would not follow my higher purpose and I would also burn out. He gets things done, but he never examines whether, or why, they need doing. Often he does things because he was told to as a child. We discuss this more in the section on schemas and introjects in the main book _Life Awakening_.

This is where the Wise Woman and the Tree come in to help bring balance with their insight into the bigger picture. None of my sub-personalities are good or bad, they are just me. I can't have them evicted; my only option is to dialogue with them, to negotiate and to get them to work together so I can continue on my path.

Using the Inner Voice preparation exercise again, just allow your characters to form in your mind as you meditate. You might like to take a journey along a path to the house where they live, visiting each in turn, noticing them, asking their names. Following this exercise, take note of when these characters emerge in your daily life.

Write down the names of your characters and what they are like below and what that experience was like for you.

Continuing our Archetype Work

Caroline Myss (2001) suggests:
Imagine each archetype sitting in a chair across from you, and ask the questions directly to the archetype. You can even write a letter to the archetype if you find that more agreeable, asking the same questions in writing. Allow the archetype to respond, the answers coming from the deepest levels of your own intuition. Or simply ask yourself, and wait for the answer to come to you. Here are some sample questions:

- What events or personal characteristics led me to choose this archetype?

- How long has this archetypal pattern been a part of my life?

- What role has this archetype played for me?

- Which prominent people have interacted with the aspect of my nature supported by this archetype? (For instance, if it's the Teacher archetype, think of the people who have played important roles in your own education or inspired you to be a teacher to others.)

- What relationship might it have to my personal unfinished business - to those people I haven't forgiven, or to events in the past that I can't let go of? And might this archetype now help me in healing those situations?

- What myths, fairy tales, or spiritual stories that have meaning for me do I associate with this archetype?

- Has this archetype appeared in my dreams?

- Does thinking of this archetype make me feel empowered or disempowered?

You should also look for spiritual resonance in your archetypes. Ask yourself:

- What impact has this archetype had on my spirituality?

- What have I learned about my own shadow aspect through this archetype?

- Has it caused me to block or forgo change that needs to happen?

- What immediate guidance might this archetype have to offer me in the present moment?

Use this space to write your answers from the above exercise and to reflect on the answers.

It's time to start pulling together all the information from the three different sections. Write here the qualities you identified from your Birth Gifts, the qualities from your life so far and see if you can find the corresponding archetype.

Qualities from Birth Gifts	Qualities from Life	Archetypes that correspond

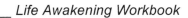

 Take time to reflect on what you have identified and what it means to you.

Presentation

We now go on to look at how we present to the world.

Client example

Here is an example of some notes we made when we first assessed "Amanda" to give an example of what we noted before beginning the details of her Now assessment.

When we first trialled HTP we began with Now and then worked back to Birth Gifts so this was a first session.

What we observed in presentation:
Amanda arrived punctually, smart-casual dressed in a turquoise jacket, wearing make-up, hair recently dyed and straightened and showing attention to detail in her presentation. This fits with presentation being important, as we discovered when talking to her.

She was chatty, smiley and had an engaging tone of voice. She was personable and made small talk. She knew how to be sociable and took some responsibility for the conversation. There was a degree of nervousness (to be expected given the situation). She kept this positive, interested demeanor up through most of the session and it took longer for recognition of anxiety and upset which was not shown initially. (This links to her beliefs about some parts of her being acceptable and others which aren't.)

She was receptive to what we said and the conversation flowed.

She maintained eye contact and she moved and flowed; she used gestures and hand movements. She walked into the room without visible stuckness in her movement and body, as if her body was joined up. We saw that she was energetic within her body but there was a cognitive interruption to her energy in some areas. She would push down certain types of energy, seeing them as less desirable.

She did report tight shoulders; this may be part of the physical manifestation of the energy repression and holding in of her excitement. We discussed excitement and energy in childhood and her beliefs around it.

Imaginary session

Have a think about how you are today. Imagine walking into the therapy room and maybe meeting with Miriam and Jill.

What would you be wearing?
How would you walk?
Would you be casual and relaxed, or fully made up and manicured?

There is no right way to be, we are looking at who YOU are.

What colours do you wear?
What details might we notice?
How likely is it that you would arrive on time, early or late?

Don't judge, be real.

If you imagine taking a seat in this imaginary room, which seat would it be and why?
What might draw your attention in the room?
Would you take off your coat, or sit on the edge of your seat?
Would you curl your feet under you or fold your arms?

How might you talk, what is the quality of your voice?
What do you talk about?
What words do you use about yourself?
Do you use your hands and body and face when you talk or not?
What expressions or phrases do you use?
What do you like, or not like, to see in us as we talk with you?
What puts you off or makes you feel at home?

How would you describe yourself to us at this point in your life?
What problems, worries or concerns might your bring?
What would you want therapy to solve or resolve?

Reflect on how others might see you and now reflect on how this initial picture of you shows us your unique triquetra of Mind-Body-Spirit.

For now just close your eyes and imagine the session.

Write about your presentation at your imaginary session. What does this tell you about you? What might others see? Does this impression / presentation help you, or not?

Fill out the table, jotting down ideas and notes from your imaginary session.

Think about what you will be wearing: colours worn, neat or loose, tidy, scruffy, care and time...

What words will you use? Will you talk much? ....

Voice: bubbly, flat, quiet? Finished sentences? ....

What will you see and notice (if anything)? ....

Actions: still body or moving? ....

Will you be punctual? ....

Are you able to make requests (for example, Can I use the toilet? Should I take my shoes off?) ....?

What else can you think of when you first meet other people? ....

Psychological Now

We are now going to guide you through an assessment of where your Mind-Body-Spirit is now. To begin we will look at where you are in terms of your mind, or your 'psychological now'. We will ask you to reflect on any worries or thought patterns you have and we will explore your unique 'make and model' further through lenses such as a Myers Briggs questionnaire and the Enneagram.

Seeker's own Description

Something has brought you to the Life Awakening course and workbook. Throughout this course you will have returned to this question, meditated and journalled about it. Taking all you have discovered, what concerns do you have about how you feel emotionally, the thoughts and worries, the beliefs that hold you back?

Myers Briggs

Now for a different perspective on archetypes, Carl Jung decided there were four ways of perceiving the world and the combinations of these make up 16 different personality types. The Myers Briggs is based on those 16 personality types. Have a look at yourself from this perspective. The full Myers Briggs questionnaire is best done with an expert, but for a general idea and pattern you might like to simply use a free online questionnaire.

 There are many websites that enable you to identify your Myers-Briggs, use one now.

Miriam's example

- Moderate preference of Extraversion over Introversion
- Moderate preference of Sensing over Intuition
- Strong preference of Feeling over Thinking
- Moderate preference of Judging over Perceiving

Guardians of birthdays, holidays and celebrations, ESFJs are generous entertainers. They enjoy and joyfully observe traditions and are liberal in giving.

ESFJs enjoy being in charge. They see problems clearly and delegate easily, work hard and play with zest. They willingly provide service (which embodies life's meaning) and expect the same from others.

ESFJs are easily wounded. And when wounded, their emotions will not be contained. They by nature 'wear their hearts on their sleeves', often exuding warmth and bonhomie, but not infrequently boiling over with the vexation of their souls.

As caretakers, ESFJs sense danger all around - germs within, the elements without, unscrupulous malefactors, insidious character flaws. The world is a dangerous place, not to be trusted. Not that the ESFJ is paranoid; hyper-vigilant would be more precise. And thus they serve excellently as protectors, outstanding in fields such as medical care and elementary education.

Use this space to write what your Myers Briggs type is, what the characteristics are and how you feel about the results. Does it sound like you?

Enneagram

Enneagram encompasses the spirituality of grasping our own psychology. The Enneagram has nine different personality types. Each type has a soul journey to make in order to return to wholeness. The Enneagram, similar to Myers Briggs, uses a questionnaire to help determine which of the nine different personality types you are. The Enneagram Institute offers some concise and clear descriptions of your type once you have discovered it.

This process, like Myers Briggs, is usually best done within a group session with a trained Enneagram facilitator, as it is more complex, but for a general idea and pattern you might like to simply use a free online questionnaire.

 There are many websites that enable you to identify your Enneagram.

Miriam has included her Enneagram type – The Helper – type 2.

Involved, socially aware, usually extroverted, twos are the type of people who remember everyone's birthday and who go the extra mile to help out a co-worker, spouse or friend in need.

People of this personality type essentially feel that they are worthy in so far as they are helpful to others. Love is their highest ideal. Selflessness is their duty. Giving to others is their reason for being.

Twos are warm, emotional people who care a great deal about their personal relationships, devote an enormous amount of energy to them, and who expect to be appreciated for their efforts. They are practical people who thrive in the helping professions and who know how to make a home comfortable and inviting. Helping others makes twos feel good about themselves, being needed makes them feel important, being selfless makes twos feel virtuous.

Twos often develop a sense of entitlement when it comes to the people closest to them. Because they have extended themselves for others, they begin to feel that gratitude is owed to them. They can become intrusive and demanding if their often unacknowledged emotional needs go unmet. They can be bossy and manipulative, feeling entirely justified in being so, because they 'have earned the right' and their intentions are good. The darkest side of the type two fixation appears when the two begins to feel that they will never receive the love they deserve for all of their efforts. Under such circumstances, they can become hysterical, irrational and even abusive.

Because twos are generally helping others meet their needs, they can forget to take care of their own. This can lead to physical burnout, emotional exhaustion and emotional volatility. Twos need to learn that they can only be of true service to others if they are healthy, balanced and centered in themselves.

Use this space to write what your Enneagram type is, what the characteristics are and how you feel about the results. Does it sound like you?

Can you see how similar Miriam's Enneagram results and Myers Briggs type are? One is called the Caregiver and the other the Helper! Amanda was also Caregiver but her Enneagram was Loyalist – you can read more about how this showed in her life in the case studies in our *Life Awakening* book.

Can you see how our personality types match each other and fascinatingly, how they correspond to our Birth Gifts charts?

 Write some key words that stand out for you from these two tests.

Compare the results in the space below.

Myers Briggs - adjectives	Enneagram - adjectives

In HTP we prefer not to use modern psychiatric terms, or indeed any labels that define a person. We are using labels to explore and play. Unfortunately modern psychiatric labels can cause harm because these are seen as a person's identity rather than clues as to understanding uniqueness.

However, in the world we live in most people are familiar with certain terms and use them in everyday language: words like depressed, eating disorder, anxiety disorder, obsessive-compulsive disorder and so on. What other labels might a professional have applied to you or people within your circle: labels such as autistic, dyslexic, ADHD, helpful, sweet, clever or good for example?

 Have you or anyone else used these types of labels about yourself?

Put them here, if you want to.

Reflect on the usefulness of these labels to you; sometimes it is helpful for example to know that your reactions and feelings are completely normal.

Would you like to cross any of these labels out now?

Would you like to re-write these labels in a way that more accurately expresses you? For example, 'I love moving from project to project.' or 'I like to be organised'.

Beliefs and Introjects

Beliefs and rules are those thoughts we have about ourselves, the world and other people. They develop in childhood and come with us into later life. Some are useful, such as, 'Don't run across the road without looking!' Others are less helpful such as believing the negative messages we received as a child, for example, 'I'm stupid, I'm worthless, I'm no good' etc.

Some we can connect to quite quickly and some are more deeply buried. The work we did on your growing up should give you some insight into the beliefs and rules you have. The section in our main *Life Awakening* book takes this work deeper.

Make a list of your beliefs in the box below – leave some space in between for a later part of the exercise.

My core beliefs and life rules are:

Take some coloured pens, and cross out or rewrite any of the beliefs or life rules you no longer wish to keep.

Write about how these exercises were for you.

Environmental Stressors

It is a well-known fact that certain environmental factors impact on us and cause us stress, such as moving home, divorce or bereavement.

What are the stressors in your life at the moment and how are you managing them? Are you a problem solver seeing a way to resolve them, a list maker of things to do or do you put your head in the sand and avoid thinking about it?

Life stressor	How you respond to your problems

 Write your thoughts about the current stressors when you look at your environment from your Viewing Platform and how you manage them. Does relaxing and using the Viewing Platform help? Does your Inner Voice have any messages for you?

Look back at the three sections, Birth Gifts, Life Themes and Patterns and Now. Complete the table identifying any common factors and the main learning points.

Birth Gifts	Life Themes and Patterns	Now

Inner Voice Meditation

In our journey to find 'you' and your life, you may have been told by others in your life about who you are and during this course picked up more adjectives such as astrologers' descriptions of how you are. Now it's time for you to work it out. The work in this section is to help you to separate out what you have been told and what your Inner Voice says about who you are. Take some time to listen to your Inner Voice as you meditate using the Inner Voice meditation described in the beginning of this workbook.

Write about the difference between who you are and who you have been told you are.

In this section we have looked at archetypes, presentation, Myers Briggs, Enneagram, beliefs and introjects and environmental stressors. In the next section we will explore your connection with your body.

The Physical Now

Seeker's Own Description

In this section about the body we will guide you through an HTP body assessment.

The body in the Now part of this course is primarily experiential and usually takes place on the HTP workshops, with many exercises and some hands-on work.

If you are undertaking this course as home study there are a few online questionnaires and exercises you can do on the resource page of the website. You may also wish to visit a body practitioner of your own choosing. Maybe the Alexander Technique, Zero Balancing, massage, acupuncture or osteopathy appeal to you? Please ask your Inner Voice.

Opening Meditation

> *Breathe in and out, let your mind scan your body from the top of your head, down through your head and neck ...*
> *Scan your shoulders, down through your arms and fingers ...*
> *Let your mind scan your chest, stomach and pelvic areas ...*
> *Connect with your legs, your knees, your feet and toes.*
>
> *Now listen to your body.*
> *Which part of your body is trying to say hello?*
> *Which part would like you to pay it some attention?*
>
> *Focus your attention on this part of your body and say 'hello'.*
> *Then work the rest of your body saying 'hello' to all the different areas.*

How was it to practise reconciliation with your body in that exercise?

 How would you describe your physical health in your own words?

Physical Assessment of Body Input and Output

In the Human Trinity Principles we think of our bodies as being given input and giving us output. For example input might be diet, drugs, exercise. Output is what we experience from our body; this might include aches, pains, illnesses, weight gain or loss.

Complete this chart as honestly as you can. Be gentle to yourself, the results may surprise you.

Input	Comment
Diet	
Drugs	
Exercise	
Chemicals	
Grooming	
Sleep	
Connection to and awareness of body	

Now for output

Output	Comment
Aches and Pains	
Illness	
Symptoms	
Fitness	
Other	

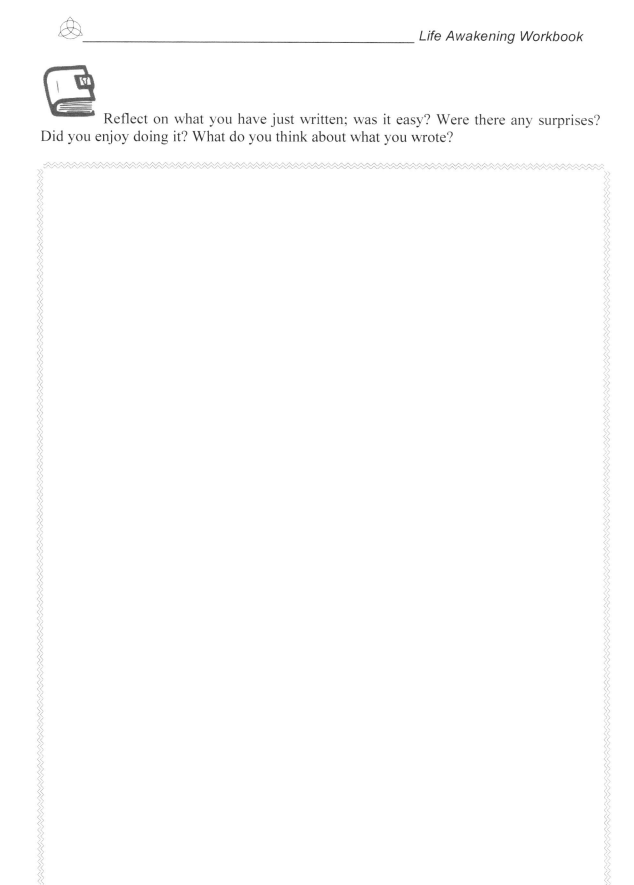

Reflect on what you have just written; was it easy? Were there any surprises? Did you enjoy doing it? What do you think about what you wrote?

Louise Hay and the Root Causes

Louise Hay (1984) wrote the book *You Can Heal Your Life*. This is based on her insights into the relationship between the mind and the body. Exploring the way that limiting thoughts and ideas control and constrict us, she offers a key to understanding the roots of our physical diseases and discomforts. While it can seem simplistic to ascribe a thought to an illness, she claims that practitioners who use her book report that the underlying cause she cites is 90% accurate in terms of bodily symptoms and the spiritual or psychological problem underpinning these symptoms.

HTP does not state whether thoughts cause these symptoms or not. What it does state is always ask your Inner Voice to decide whether the information given is helpful to you or not. This is another lens that may be helpful to you in exploring your body's 'Now'.

There is a lot of research and more information on how thoughts can affect the body in our core book to be published in 2015. Miriam's blog, 'Mind Magic' (http://www.blue-skies.org.uk/mind-magic/) or review of her Body-Mind workshop with Imogen Ragone (http://www.blue-skies.org.uk/training/) are also available on the internet.

Example of cause and affirmation

According to Louise Hay, migraine headaches are created by people who want to be perfect and who create a lot of pressure on themselves. They may have a dislike of being driven or be resisting the flow of life.

'Headaches come from invalidating the self. The next time you get a headache, stop and ask yourself where and how you have just made yourself wrong. Forgive yourself, let it go, and the headache will dissolve back into the nothingness from where it came.'

Louise Hay's recommended affirmation:

" I relax into the flow of life and let life provide all that I need easily and comfortably.

Life is for me."

If you have a physical condition such as asthma, arthritis or headaches, look up Louise Hay's explanation for this illness and write it down here.

Now reflect upon this information and decide using your Inner Voice whether this is useful to you or not.

If you feel after listening to your Inner Voice that Louise's reason is not helpful information for you, please write in the box below your condition and what you feel is the reason for your condition.

Next write out the affirmation appropriate for this condition, either use Louise Hay's or design your own based on your Inner Voice's reason for your condition.

Condition	Affirmation

It is not always easy to do this work. There are many blocks, including self blame (which is not appropriate or helpful) and there can be various reasons for illness, many of which we do not know or understand.

If exploring the reason for your physical problems becomes distressing or you find that you are blaming yourself in some way, please speak to someone who can support you.

HTP does not blame people for their suffering; it simply aims to understand the message behind suffering. Often in understanding the message we can help ourselves back onto our path and this gives us renewed energy and health. We are a trinity and central to our model is the idea that when we are connected to our life purpose our Mind-Body-Spirit Trinity works more smoothly. In many traditions suffering is the route to enlightenment and produces compassionate people.

Let's look at what is happening in your life and how this impacts on your body.

 Fill out the following worksheet:

	Comment
Age	
Relationships	
Work	
Home	
Extended family	
Other	

Meditate upon the relationship between what is happening in your life and your physical health.

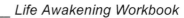

 How do you feel your environment and lifestyle affect your physical health?

 What bodywork have you had in the past, if any? What bodywork do you respond to well? Why is this?

Movement and the Self

Now we are going to look in more depth at how you move and your relationship to movement. To do that reflect on the following questions: How do you move and sit? Do you know? What do you think about the way you move? You can do this exercise with a friend.

Chinese Five-Elements

Miriam Says: One of the reasons I began this journey over ten years ago (connecting physical health to psychological and mental health) was my fascination when I discovered that my acupuncturist understood my psychology through his lens!

My element, Earth was diagnosed by my acupuncturist through the way my voice sounds, the colour of my tongue and my bodily ailments. Interestingly the key characteristics of Earth all point to:

- Mothering and caring
- Not asking but expecting
- Expressing needs a lot
- Homemaking

Physical problems in the Earth type often relate to the stomach, food, nurture, nourishment and the spleen.

Can you see how well this fits my Myers Briggs type of the Caregiver and my Enneagram type of the Helper? Remember also my Birth Gifts: sun sign being Cancer (the universal mother), my tarot cards being about relationships?

The best person to help you decide your five-element type is, of course, a qualified five-element acupuncturist, however you can take an online questionnaire, which should give you a rough idea.

Take a quiz to find your Chinese element type and write it here.

Reflect on whether that seems right for you. If yes, why? If not, why? Which would you choose?

A very generalised overview to the types is below.

Read and research.

Fire: The Inspirer. Their strengths include awakening the potential and aliveness in others. Fires are influencing and enthusiastic.

Earth: The Diplomat. Their strengths include caring for ourselves and others. They balance between giving and receiving.

Wood: The Leader. The strengths of people strong in the wood element include exploring the unknown, being innovative, adaptive and expansive.

Metal: The Observer. Their strengths include detached observation, providing the structure for transformation.

Water: The Philosopher. Their strengths include bringing light to what is hidden through reflection and renewal.

Body Care

 Looking at your body, make a list of the body care you would like to give yourself. It doesn't need to be a long list, realistic is far more useful.

Body Care Worksheet

Body part	Care you would like to give

You may wish to talk this through with someone else so that they can help you come up with ideas about what your body needs. At all times do not do what other people are doing, but what your Inner Voice tells you.

Note in the table the areas of your body you really like and why.

Areas of your body you like	Why you like them

Gratitude to your body.

Thank you feet for walking.

Thank you ....   for.........

Thank you ....   for.........

Thank you ....   for.........

Thank you ....   for.........

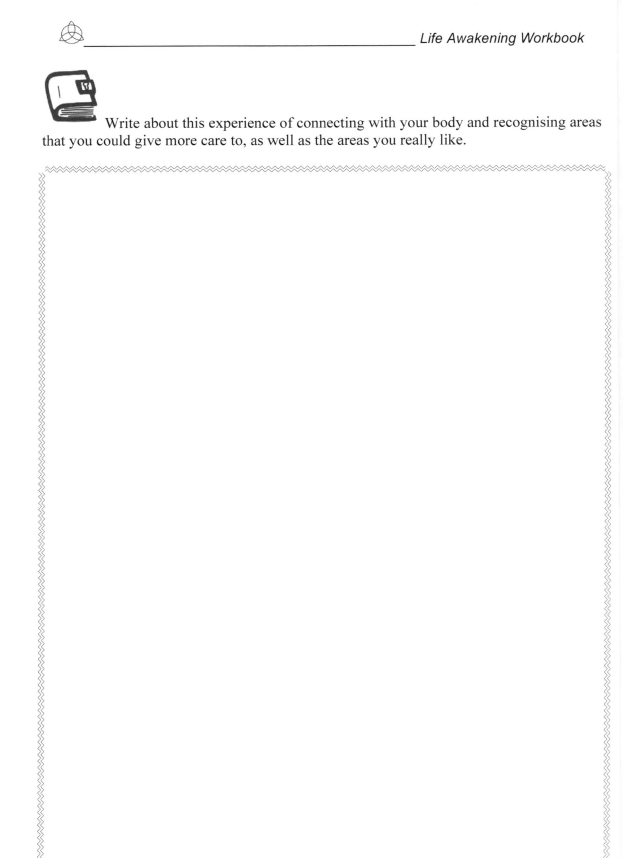

Write about this experience of connecting with your body and recognising areas that you could give more care to, as well as the areas you really like.

To complete the body exercises, use the space below to create for yourself some body affirmations.

Body Affirmations Exercise

Say these affirmations out loud three times each day for one week.

Reflect on how this section of the workbook was for you. Did you enjoy it? Did you skip parts? Was this section more difficult or boring for you? What does it mean if it was? Did you really enjoy it? Did saying affirmations for a week have a result?

Well done, you have completed the body section. The next part focuses on spirit.

Spiritual Now

In conclusion to this whole Life Awakening review we're now going to look at your spiritual experience of Now.

Central to the Human Trinity Principles is the concept that a person is made up of mind, body and energy and that these three parts all interlink and affect each other.

When a person is connected with their sense of purpose and on their path they feel a sense of well-being and energy. There is much more about this within our main book, where we call this Life Purpose Regulation Function.

Just take note of what your current spiritual practice is and any measures you have you taken to develop a spiritual practice.

Seeker's Own Description

Energy is an important part of HTP. Some people feel their energy really easily, others only notice it when they collapse.

Do you notice your energy? And if so, how do you feel your energy is right now?

An energy assessment is best undertaken with a qualified energy worker. It can be undertaken with an HTP practitioner, on a workshop or in a drop-in session. There are more details and information on energy assessment and experiencing your own energy (chi, prana, life force) within our longer book.

Chakras

Chakras are one way to understand our energy systems and identify where energy is flowing freely and the areas where it is stuck. The different chakras are linked to different developmental ages, areas of your body and emotions. We include further information about chakras in the main book.

 There are a number of websites where you can undertake a chakra test.

 Incorporate the findings into the table below.

Chakra	Does it flow freely?	Does it need work and if so what ideas do you have to work with it?
Crown		
Third Eye		
Throat		
Heart		
Solar Plexus		
Sacral		
Base (Root)		

What do you think about the results of your chakra test?

Dream and Intuit your Destiny

Life Purpose Meditation

In order to connect with your life purpose, which is the conclusion of all this work, you will undertake a Life Purpose Meditation. The clues to the path that will bring you the most fulfilment are all there. Your inner self has listened to all the work you have done so far and has assimilated a lifetime of mind, body and spirit experience. Don't put pressure on your brain to come up with a life purpose, just gently connect with what you already know. Over the Life Awakening programme you have developed your Inner Voice, which has loosened and opened to allow more thoughts, ideas and intuitions to inform you. You have strengthened your capacity to listen to your Inner Voice. Now prepare for the meditation by once again accessing your Viewing Platform (described at the beginning of The Workbook) and then allowing your mind to wander through these questions. Enjoy seeing yourself and connecting with yourself.

   Undertake the following meditation; once you have done it write your results in the table below.

General relaxation

The activities I now love are…
My jobs are / have been…
My best qualities are…
The qualities I would like to develop are…
I shine when I…
I excel at…
I am most myself / happiest / feel at home when…
What I do effortlessly is…
I keep being drawn to…

 Reflect on the following questions:

Do you feel you are on your path or stuck or directionless?

Quickly and with little thought, what would you be in a parallel universe?

Looking at the patterns of your life, your archetypes, characteristics and adjectives, what do you seem to be?

 Ask yourself:

What or who am I living my life for?

Consider now whether there are choices you need to make in your life journey. What are the next steps in this process?

Are there things you need to accept in your life or are there things that need to change? What are the next steps in this process?

Now ask yourself what is my next step in my life journey? How can I allow this process? How can I follow the voice of my soul? How can I sing my heart's song?

What do I really need to make this my life, now?

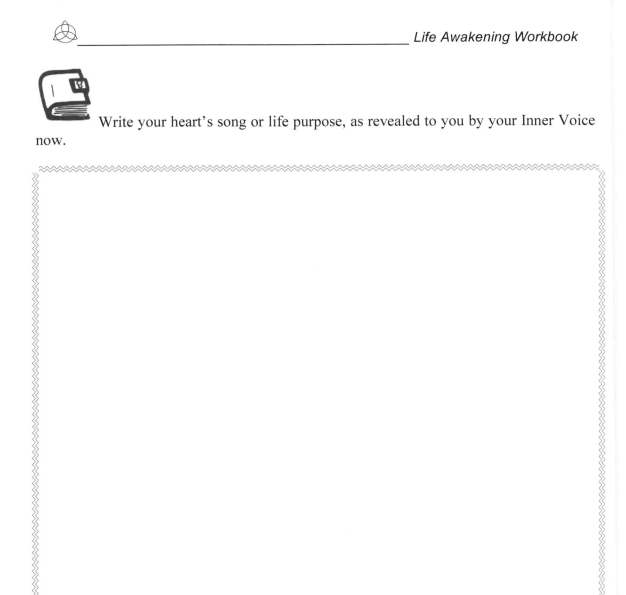

Write your heart's song or life purpose, as revealed to you by your Inner Voice now.

In order to maintain all the work that you have done throughout this course one of the most important things to remember will be the accessibility of your Inner Voice at all times.

 Reflect on your sense of Self. Ask yourself these questions:

Where is my Self located?

What is the source of my energy?

Is my sense of presence within or without my body?

Write about your sense of presence, source or Self and your own spiritual awareness.

Conclusion to Part Three

Well done, you have reached the end of the final part of your life review. In this section you have reviewed your mind, your personality styles and thinking patterns, you have explored your relationship with your body and connected with your energy systems.

So the final part of the workbook is about what to do next.

Your Life Review - What to do Next

You have reviewed your life, from the wonderful possibilities given to you in your Birth Gifts, through your life story's unfolding themes and patterns and to a current evaluation of yourself in the Now.

You have gained a stronger relationship with the wise man or wise woman within you through listening to your Inner Voice, you have been able to use your thinking through accessing your Viewing Platform and you have been able to engage your bodily sensing and emotional feelings through exercises.

So why did we undertake such a comprehensive and full life review?

The Human Trinity Principles are based on the triquetra model of mind, body and spirit. We believe that when our life purpose is on track, our energy, our mind and our body all function better, connect up and flow.

As we said at the start of this course, the more we try to be who we are not, the more frustrated and disheartened we become. Now you have completed this review you know who you are!

In order to feel more peaceful, more fulfilled and happier all you need to do is to be you!

Remembering your learning through the course and connecting with your Inner Voice can be used from moment to moment. For example, you can decide whether you want to lie down or go for a walk, and you can listen to your Inner Voice in terms of the bigger choices in life, relating to the relationships and the career that you choose.

This section is entitled, 'What to do next.' Human Trinity Principles state that what you need to do next is to be yourself fully and joyously, with acceptance and understanding, compassion and a good sense of humour!

Connect with your Inner Voice peacefully.

Write in the different columns what your Inner Voice has directed you to understand and know about your Mind-Body-Spirit. What ideas does your Inner Voice have for restoring or maintaining your balance?

Mind	Body	Spirit

Summarise and reflect on your life journey so far; incorporate all the different parts of your life review.

Maintenance

Do you feel that your Inner Voice is strong enough and available enough to support you in following your path and your destiny?

The Life Awakening review will have given you a better understanding of where you are blocked and what work you need to enable you to flow, whether that's psychotherapy, bodywork, or a more spiritual, energetic approach.

Closing Meditation

Return to your Viewing Platform…. Review and look over the whole of this course from where you were at the beginning and through to the end now.

Look right over to the edge of your landscape, maybe to the mountains; see if you can see the path of the future ahead…

Relax. Pay attention to any voices, symbols or affirmations that come to you on your Viewing Platform now.

 Continue to dream and intuit your destiny and to regularly ask your Inner Voice for the answers that you need.

AFTERWORD

We hope you have enjoyed this workbook and reviewing your life. What an incredible journey your life has been so far, and we hope this Life Awakening process has deepened your appreciation of all that has gone into the making of you.

Being you is what you can do most easily, trying to be who you are not, as discussed at the start, causes stresses and problems and discontent.

We hope this has inspired you to be more you and that you will find the results of this to be profound. The support to 'Be You' continues in our other books, our websites and social media.

If you wish to continue on your journey with the Human Trinity Principles you may wish to attend one of our courses or read the _Life Awakening_ book. We love hearing from those who have woken up with Life Awakening.

It has been a pleasure to be your guides on this journey.

Enjoy being you!

Jillian and Miriam 2014

Further Reading

Abraham, S. (1994). *How To Read The Tarot.* Woodbury: Llewellyn Publications.

Adrienne, C. (1998). *The Purpose of Your Life.* New York: Eagle Brook.

Almaas, A. H. (1988). *The Pearl Beyond Price.* Berkeley, California: Diamond Books.

Bach, R. (1972). *Jonathan Livingston Seagull.* London: Turnstone Press Ltd.

Beisser, A (1970). *The Paradoxical Theory of Change.* The Gestalt Journal Press.

Berens, L. V. & Nardi, D. (1999). *The 16 Sixteen Personality Types.* Huntington Beach, California: Telos Publications.

Bourne, C. (2007). *Five Gateways.* Milton Keynes: Openhand Foundation.

Bradshaw, J. (1993). *Creating Love.* London: Judy Piakus (Publishers) Ltd.

Briggs Myers, I., (1985). *Manual*: *A Guide to the Development and Use of the Myers-Briggs Type Indicator.* Palo Alto, California: Consulting Psychologists Press, Inc.

Brown, B. (1999). *Soul without Shame.* Boston & London: Shambhala Publications, Inc.

Chopra, D. (1990). *Perfect Health.* New York: Bantam Books.

Chopra, D. (1996). *The Seven Spiritual Laws Of Success.* London: Bantam Press.

Dolowich G. (2003). *Archetypal Acupuncture.* Aptos, California: Jade Mountain Publishing.

Dowrick, S. (1997). *Forgiveness and Other Acts of Love.* London: The Women's Press.

Ernst, S & Goodison, L. (1981). *In Our Own Hands.* London: The Women's Press Limited.

Freud, S. (1962). *Two Short Accounts of Psycho-Analysis.* London: Pelican Books.

Gerwick-Brodeur, M. & Lenard, L. (2007). *The Complete Idiot's Guide to Astrology.* New York: Penguin Group.

Gladwell, M. (2005). *Blink.* London: Penguin Group.

Gleason, B & M. (2012). *Exceptional Relationships.* Bloomington: iUniverse, Inc.

Greenfield, P M. (2009). *Unravelling.* UK: True Alignment.

Hay, L. (1984). Y*ou Can Heal Your Life,* Hay House Inc.

Hicks, A. & J. (1999). *Healing your Emotions.* London: Thorsons.

Hirsh, S. & Kummerow, J. (1989). *Life Types.* New York: Warner Books, Inc.

Holden, R. (2013). *Loveability.* London: Hay House.

Hollis, J. (2006). *Finding Meaning In The Second Half Of Life.* New York: Penguin Group.

Hollis, J. (1993). *The Middle Passage.*

Huan, Z & Rose, K. (1995). *Who can Ride the Dragon?* Massachusetts: Paradigm Publications.

Israel, M. (1981). *The Pain That Heals.* Guernsey: The Guernsey Press Company Limited.

Jampolsky, G. (1979). *Love Is Letting Go Of Fear.* Berkeley, California: Celestial Arts.

Johnson, S.M. (1985). *Characterological Transformation.* New York. London: W. W Norton & Company.

Keyes, M. (1988). *Emotions and the Enneagram.* Muir Beach, California: Molysdatur Publications.

Kohanov, L. (2001). *The Tao of Equus.* Novato, California: New World Library.

Kornfield, J. (1993). *A Path With Heart.* PLACE: Bantam Books.

Krieger, R.N. (1986). *The Therapeutic Touch.* New York: Prentice Hall Press.

Monbourquette, J. (1997). *How To Befriend Your Shadow.* Canada: Novalis.

Parfitt, W. (2003). *Psychosynthesis: The Elements and Beyond.* Glastonbury: PS Avalon.

Peck, S.M. (1983). *The Road Less Travelled.* London: Hutchinson, Random House.

Peirce, P. (2009). *Frequency.* New York: Atria Books.

Rosenberg, M.B. (2003). *Nonviolent Communication: A Language of Life.* Encinitas: PuddleDancer Press.

Rosengarten, A. (2000). *Tarot and Psychology.* St Paul, Minnesota: Paragon House.

Rubenfield, I. (2000). *The Listening Hand.* New York: Bantam Books.

Sedgwick, D. (1994). *The Wounded Healer.* London: Routledge.

Shaw, R. (2003). *The Embodied Psychotherapist.* East Sussex: Brunner-Routledge.

Simpson, L. (1999). *The Book of Chakra Healing.* UK: Gaia Books.

Steiner, G. (1989). *Real Presences.* London: The University of Chicago Press.

Storr, A. (1988). *Solitude.* London: Flamingo.

Storr, A. (1998). *The Essential Jung.* London: Fontana Press.

Totton, N & Jacobs, M. (2001). *Character and Personality Types.* Buckingham: Open University Press.

Virtue, D. (1998). *Chakra Clearing.* New York: Hay House, Inc,

Webb, K. (1996). *The Enneagram.* London: HarperCollins Publishers.

Wosket, V. (1999). *The Therapeutic Use Of Self.* East Sussex: Routledge.

Yalom, I.D. (1989). *Love's Executioner.* London: Penguin Group.

Authors' Biographies

Miriam Grace, MA, MBACP, UKCP Reg. Psychotherapist, Senior Accred. BACP Therapist, Senior Accred. BACP Supervisor, University Lecturer, Trainer, Coach, Mentor, Director of Blue Skies (established 1990), Co-Creator of the Human Trinity Principles (established 2012)

Miriam has been practising as a psychotherapist for over twenty-five years. She has a fully-subscribed, private psychotherapy practice, seeing clients, running therapy groups and workshops and providing clinical supervision, teaching and training for other therapists. She has taught on psychotherapy courses at Nottingham and Derby Universities and has had contracts to train within HM Prison Services, Social Services, Rape Crisis Centres, NHS and AddAction among many.

Miriam co-founded the Inner Voice Meditation group and written and run workshops with Jillian from Soulistic Therapy on their *Life Awakening* programme. They are in the final stages of writing a book based on the Human Trinity Principles and the *Life Awakening* Programme and this is their first associated workbook.

Miriam incorporates her experience in psychosynthesis, reiki, card readings, zero balancing and kinesiology into her work. She is also a Laughter Yoga Leader and her weekly Laughter and Happiness group integrates her own psychotherapeutic ideas and mindfulness into the framework of Laughter Yoga.

www.blue-skies.org.uk

Jillian Schofield, MSc Cog. Beh. Psych. MSc Psych. Couns. PGCert, Inter-Prof. Ed. BSc (Hons) Psych. EMDR. FHEA. BABCP Accredited Practitioner, Trainer and clinical Supervisor. University Lecturer, Trainer, Coach, Mentor, Director of Soulistic therapy, Co-Creator of the Human Trinity Principles

Jillian is the founder of Soulistic Therapy based in Derby, UK, where she offers healing in the form of integrative psychotherapy, cognitive behavioural psychotherapy, group psychotherapy, EMDR, shamanic healing, energy healing and angelic reiki. She also offers clinical and research supervision. She is a Laughter Yoga instructor. She offers training on the above-mentioned approaches and co-facilitates the *Life Awakening* workshops with Miriam.

Jillian works at the University of Derby as a Senior Lecturer and the College Lead for Learning Enhancement in the College of Health and Social Care. She has program led a number of psychotherapy programmes, at both undergraduate and postgraduate levels. Jillian has lectured on a number of psychotherapy programmes, both adult and child related. She had been a liaison tutor with psychotherapy courses in Greece, Scandinavia and has taught students in Israel. She is a Fellow of the Higher Educational Academy.

Jillian is the co-creator, with Miriam Grace, of Human Trinity Principles and the Inner Voice Meditation Group, co-author of *Life Awakening* and *Life Awakening the Workbook* and co-trainer on the accompanying workshops.

She is a dog lover with two gorgeous Bassett Hounds, Dotty Daydream and Maisey Moo.

www.soulistic-therapy.co.uk

Printed in Great Britain
by Amazon.co.uk, Ltd.,
Marston Gate.